WHAT'S COOKING
chicken

Tom Bridge

THUNDER BAY
P·R·E·S·S

First published in the United States in 1999 by
Thunder Bay Press
An imprint of the Advantage Publishers Group
5880 Oberlin Drive
San Diego, CA 92121-4794
www.advantagebooksonline.com

Library of Congress Cataloging in Publication Data.
Bridge, Tom.
    What's cooking Chicken / Tom Bridge.
        p.   cm.
    ISBN 1-57145-180-3
    1. Cookery, (Chicken)   I. Title   II. Title: Chicken.
TX750.5.C45B75   1999
641.6.65--dc21   98-56393
                                                                          CIP

Printed in China

4 5 00 01 02

Produced by Haldane Mason, London

Acknowledgments

Art Director: Ron Samuels
Editorial Director: Sydney Francis
Managing Editor: Jo-Anne Cox
Editorial Assistant: Elizabeth Towers
Design: dap ltd
Photography: St John Asprey
Home Economist: Jacqueline Bellefontaine
North American Managing Editor: JoAnn Padgett
North American Project Editor: Elizabeth McNulty

The publishers would like to thank the British Chicken Information Service for providing the recipes on pages 14–17, 38–41, 44, 48, 52, 58, 64, 70–75, 78–83, 88–93, 96–101, 104, 112, 116, 122, 130, 134, 138, 142, 148, 152–159, 162, 166, 170, 174–181, 184–187, 192–225, 228–233, 236–241, 244, 248–255

Note

Unless otherwise stated, milk is assumed to be full fat, eggs are medium, and pepper is freshly ground black pepper.
Front cover: Broiled Chicken with Pesto Toasts (pages 208-209)
Back cover: Sticky Chicken Drumsticks with Mango Salsa (pages 40-41)

Contents

Introduction   4

Soups & Snacks   6

Quick Dishes   68

Casseroles & Roasts   110

Barbecues & Broils   190

Spicy Dishes   222

Index   256

Introduction

Chicken has become justly popular around the world and plays an important part in the modern diet, being reasonably priced and nutritionally sound. A versatile meat, it lends itself to an enormous range of cooking methods and cuisines. Its unassertive flavor means that it is equally suited to cooking with both sweet and savory flavors. Because it has a low fat content, especially without the skin, it is an ideal meat for low cholesterol and calorie-controlled diets. As well as being an excellent source of protein, chicken contains valuable minerals, such as potassium and phosphorus, and some of the B vitamins.

COOKING METHODS FOR CHICKEN

Roasting Remove any fat from the body cavity. Rinse the bird inside and out with water, then pat dry with paper towels. Season the cavity generously with salt and pepper and add stuffing, herbs, or lemon if desired. Spread the breast of the chicken with softened butter or oil. Set on a rack in a roasting pan or shallow ovenproof dish. Roast the bird, basting two or three times with the pan juices during roasting. If the chicken is browning too quickly, cover it with foil. Test for doneness by using a meat thermometer or insert the point of a knife into the thickest part of the thigh. If the chicken is cooked, the juices will run clear with no trace of pink. Put the bird on a carving board and let rest for at least 15 minutes before serving. Make a sauce or gravy from the juices left in the roasting pan.

Broiling The intense heat of the broiler quickly seals the succulent flesh beneath a crisp, golden exterior. Place the chicken about 4–6 inches away from a moderate heat source. If the chicken seems to be browning too quickly, reduce the heat slightly. If the chicken is broiled at too high a temperature too near to the heat, the outside will burn before the inside is cooked through. If it is cooked for too long under a low heat, it will dry out. Divide the chicken into cuts to ensure even cooking. Breast meat, if cooked in one piece, can be rather dry, so it is best to cut it into chunks for kabobs. Chicken wings are best for speedy broiling.

Frying is suitable for small thighs, drumsticks, and cuts. Dry the chicken pieces with paper towels so that they brown properly and to prevent spitting during cooking. The chicken can be coated in seasoned flour, egg and bread crumbs, or a batter. Heat oil or a mixture of oil and butter in a heavy-based skillet. When the oil is very hot, add the chicken pieces, skin side down. Fry until deep golden brown all over, turning the pieces frequently during cooking. Drain well on paper towels before serving.

Sautéeing is ideal for small pieces or small birds, such as baby chickens. Heat a little oil or a mixture of oil and butter in a heavy-based skillet. Add the chicken and fry over moderate heat until golden brown, turning frequently. Add stock or other liquid, bring to a boil, then cover, and reduce the heat. Cook gently until the chicken is cooked through.

Stir-frying Skinless, boneless chicken is cut into small pieces of equal size to ensure that the meat cooks evenly and stays succulent. Preheat a wok or saucepan before adding a small amount of oil. When the oil starts to smoke, add the chicken and stir-fry with your chosen flavorings for 3–4 minutes, until cooked through. Other ingredients can be cooked at the same time, or the chicken can be cooked by itself, then removed from the wok while you stir-fry the remaining ingredients. Return the chicken to the wok once the other ingredients are cooked.

Casseroling is good for cooking cuts from larger, more mature chickens, although smaller chickens can be cooked whole. The slow cooking produces tender meat with a good flavor. Brown the chicken in butter or oil or a mixture of both. Add some stock, wine, or a mixture of both with seasonings and herbs, cover, and cook on top of the stove or in the oven until the chicken is tender. Add a selection of lightly sautéed vegetables about halfway through the cooking time.

Braising is a method which does not require liquid. The chicken pieces or a small whole chicken and vegetables are cooked together slowly in a low oven. Heat some oil in an ovenproof, flameproof casserole and gently fry the chicken until golden. Remove the chicken and fry a selection of vegetables until they are almost tender. Replace the chicken, cover tightly and cook very gently on the top of the stove or in a low oven until the chicken and vegetables are tender.

Poaching is a gentle cooking method that produces tender chicken and a stock that can be used to make a sauce to serve with the chicken. Put a whole chicken, a bouquet garni, a leek, a carrot, and an onion in a large flameproof casserole. Cover with water, season and bring to a boil. Cover and simmer for $1\frac{1}{2}$–2 hours, until the chicken is tender. Lift the chicken out, discard the bouquet garni, and use the stock to make a sauce. The vegetables can be blended to thicken the stock and served with the chicken.

FOOD SAFETY & TIPS

Chicken is liable to be contaminated by salmonella bacteria, which can cause severe food poisoning. When storing, handling, and preparing poultry, certain precautions must be observed to prevent the possibility of food poisoning.

• Check the sell-by date and best-before date. After buying, take the chicken home quickly, preferably in a freezer bag or cool box.

• Return frozen birds immediately to the freezer.

• If storing in the refrigerator, remove the wrappings and store any giblets separately. Place the chicken in a shallow dish to catch drips. Cover loosely with foil and store on the bottom shelf of the refrigerator for no more than two or three days, depending on the best before date. Avoid any contact between raw chicken and cooked food during storage and preparation. Wash your hands thoroughly after handling raw chicken.

• Prepare raw chicken on a chopping board that can be easily cleaned and bleached, such as a nonporous, plastic board.

• Frozen birds should be thawed before cooking. If there is sufficient time, thaw for about 36 hours in the refrigerator or 12 hours in a cool place. Bacteria breed in warm food at room temperature and when chicken is thawing. Cooking at high temperatures kills them. There should be no ice crystals and the flesh should feel soft and flexible. Cook the chicken as soon as possible after thawing.

• Make sure that chicken is thoroughly cooked. Test for doneness using a meat thermometer—the thigh should reach at least 175°F when cooked—or pierce the thickest part of a thigh with a knife, the juices should run clear, not pink. Never partially cook chicken, intending to complete cooking later.

CHICKEN STOCK

Chicken stock is usually made from a whole bird or wings, backs, and legs. This produces a well-flavored stock. However it can also be made using chicken bones and carcass cooked with vegetables and flavorings. Although it will not be so rich in flavor, it is still superior to stock make from a bouillon cube. A simple chicken stock can be made using giblets (except the liver, which is bitter) with a bouquet garni, onion, carrot, and some peppercorns. Homemade stock can be stored in the freezer for up to six months.

To make chicken stock: add the wings, backs, or whole chicken to a large stockpot with two quartered onions. Cook until the chicken and onions are evenly browned. Cover with cold water, bring to a boil and skim off any scum that rises to the surface. Add two chopped carrots, two chopped celery stalks, a small bunch of parsley, a few bay leaves, a thyme sprig, and a few peppercorns. Partially cover and gently simmer for about 3 hours. Strain the stock into a bowl and cool, then chill. When the stock is completely cold, remove the fat that will have set on the surface.

Soups & Snacks

Chicken soup has a long tradition of being comforting and good for us, and some cultures even think of it as a cure for all ills. It is certainly satisfying, full of flavor, and easy to digest. For the best results, use a good homemade chicken stock, although when time is at a premium, a good quality bouillon cube can be used instead. Every cuisine in the world has its own favorite version of chicken soup and in this section you'll find a selection of recipes from as far afield as Italy, Scotland, and China.

As chicken is so versatile and quick to cook, it is perfect for innovative and appetizing snacks. Its unassertive flavor means that it can be enlivened by exotic fruits and spices and Asian ingredients, such as soy sauce, sesame oil, and fresh ginger root. There are fritters, salads, and drumsticks that are stuffed and baked, or served with delicious fruity salsas. Because chicken pieces travel well and are easy to eat, many of the recipes are ideal to take on picnics or to pack in a lunch box.

Cream of Chicken & Lemon Soup

This refreshing soup with its piquant lemon flavor is perfect on summer days.

Serves 4

INGREDIENTS

4 tablespoons butter
8 shallots, thinly sliced
2 medium carrots, thinly sliced
2 stalks celery, thinly sliced
9 ounces skinless chicken breast
  meat, finely chopped

3 lemons
5 cups chicken stock
$^2/_3$ cup heavy cream
salt and pepper

sprigs of parsley and lemon slices,
  to garnish

1 Melt the butter in a large saucepan, add the vegetables and chicken, and cook gently for 8 minutes.

2 Thinly pare the lemons and blanch the lemon rind in boiling water for 3 minutes.

3 Squeeze the juice from the lemons.

4 Add the lemon rind and freshly squeezed lemon juice to the pan with the chicken stock.

5 Bring slowly to a boil and simmer for about 50 minutes. Let the soup cool, then transfer to a food processor and process until smooth. Return the soup to the saucepan, reheat, season with salt and pepper to taste, and add the heavy cream. Do not boil at this stage or the soup will curdle.

6 Transfer the soup to a warm tureen or warm individual soup bowls. Serve at once, garnished with parsley sprigs and lemon slices.

VARIATION

For an alternative citrus flavor, use 4 oranges in place of the lemons. The recipe can also be adapted to make duck and orange soup.

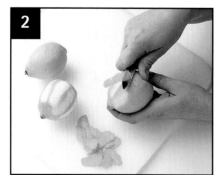

Tom's Chicken Soup

The potato has been part of the Irish diet for centuries. This recipe is originally from the north of Ireland, in the beautiful area of Moira, County Down.

Serves 4

INGREDIENTS

3 smoked bacon slices, chopped
1 pound 2 oz skinless boneless
　chicken, chopped
2 tablespoons butter
3 medium potatoes, chopped
3 medium onions, chopped

2$^1/_2$ cups giblet or
　chicken stock
2$^1/_2$ cups milk
$^2/_3$ cup heavy cream
salt and pepper

2 tablespoons chopped fresh parsley
soda bread, to serve

1 Gently fry the bacon and chicken in a large saucepan for 10 minutes.

2 Add the butter, potatoes, and onions and cook for 15 minutes, stirring all the time.

3 Add the stock and milk, then bring the soup to a boil, and simmer for 45 minutes. Season with salt and pepper to taste.

4 Blend in the cream and simmer for 5 minutes. Stir in the chopped fresh parsley, then transfer the soup to a warm tureen or individual bowls and serve with Irish soda bread.

COOK'S TIP

Soda bread is not made with yeast as bread usually is. Instead it is made with baking soda as the raising agent. It can be made with all-purpose flour or whole wheat flour.

VARIATION

For a more filling, main course soup, you can add any number of different vegetables—for example leeks, celery root, or corn.

Chicken & Leek Soup

This satisfying soup can be served as a main course.
You can add rice and bell peppers to make it even heartier, as well as colorful.

Serves 6

INGREDIENTS

12 ounces boneless chicken
12 ounces leeks
2 tablespoons butter
5 cups chicken stock

1 bouquet garni packet
8 pitted prunes, halved
salt and white pepper

cooked rice and diced bell
peppers (optional)

1 Using a sharp knife, cut the chicken and leeks into 1-inch pieces.

2 Melt the butter in a large saucepan, add the chicken and leeks, and fry for 8 minutes, stirring occasionally.

3 Add the chicken stock and bouquet garni to the mixture in the pan, and season with salt and pepper to taste.

4 Bring the soup to a boil and simmer over gentle heat for 45 minutes.

5 Add the pitted prunes with some cooked rice and diced bell peppers (if using), and simmer for 20 minutes. Remove the bouquet garni packet and discard. Pour the soup into a warm tureen or warm individual soup bowls and serve at once.

COOK'S TIP

If you have time, make the chicken stock yourself, using the recipe on page 5. Alternatively, you can buy good fresh stock from supermarkets.

COOK'S TIP

Instead of the bouquet garni packet, you can use a bunch of fresh, mixed herbs, tied together with string. Choose herbs such as parsley, thyme, and rosemary.

Thai Chicken Noodle Soup

Quick to make, this hot and spicy soup is hearty and warming. If you like your food really fiery, add a chopped dried or fresh chile with its seeds.

Serves 4-6

INGREDIENTS

1 sheet of dried egg noodles
    from a 9 ounce pack
1 tablespoon oil
4 skinless, boneless
    chicken thighs, diced
1 bunch scallions, sliced
2 garlic cloves, chopped

$^3/_4$-inch piece fresh
    ginger root, finely chopped
$3^3/_4$ cups chicken stock
scant 1 cup coconut milk
1 tablespoon red Thai
    curry paste
3 tablespoons peanut butter
2 tablespoons light soy sauce

1 small red bell pepper,
    chopped
$^1/_2$ cup frozen peas
salt and pepper

1 Put the noodles in a shallow dish and soak in boiling water following the instructions on the packet.

2 Heat the oil in a large saucepan or wok, add the chicken, and fry for 5 minutes, stirring until lightly browned. Add the white part of the scallions, the garlic, and ginger and fry for 2 minutes, stirring constantly. Add the stock, coconut milk, curry paste, peanut butter, and soy sauce. Season with salt and pepper to taste. Bring to a boil, stirring constantly, then simmer for 8 minutes, stirring occasionally. Add the red bell pepper, peas, and green scallion tops and cook for 2 minutes.

3 Add the drained noodles and heat through. Spoon into individual bowls and serve with a spoon and fork.

VARIATION

Green Thai curry paste can be used for a less fiery flavor. It is available from specialty gourmet stores.

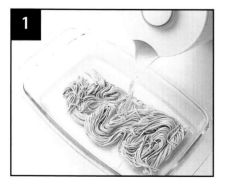

Chicken & Pasta Broth

This satisfying soup makes a good lunch or supper dish and you can use any vegetables that you have to hand. Children will love the tiny pasta shapes.

Serves 6

INGREDIENTS

12 ounces boneless
   chicken breasts
2 tablespoons sunflower oil
1 medium onion, diced
1½ cups diced carrots
9 ounces cauliflower florets

3¾ cups chicken stock
2 teaspoons dried mixed herbs
1 cup small pasta shapes
salt and pepper

Parmesan cheese (optional)
   and crusty bread, to serve

1 Using a sharp knife, finely dice the chicken, discarding any skin.

2 Heat the oil in a large saucepan and quickly sauté the chicken and vegetables until they are lightly colored.

3 Stir in the stock and herbs. Bring to a boil and add the pasta . Return to a boil, cover, and simmer for 10 minutes, stirring occasionally to prevent the pasta shapes from sticking together.

4 Season with salt and pepper to taste and sprinkle with Parmesan cheese, if using. Serve with fresh crusty bread.

COOK'S TIP

You can use any small pasta shapes for this soup—try conchigliette or ditalini, or even spaghetti broken up into small pieces. To make a fun soup for children, you could add animal-shaped or alphabet pasta.

VARIATION

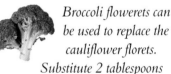

Broccoli flowerets can be used to replace the cauliflower florets. Substitute 2 tablespoons chopped fresh mixed herbs for the dried mixed herbs.

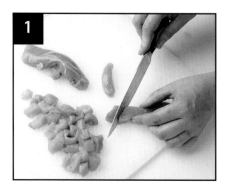

Chicken Consommé

This is a very flavorful soup, especially if you make it from real chicken stock.
Egg shells are used to give a crystal clear appearance.

Serves 8–10

INGREDIENTS

8 cups chicken stock
²/₃ cup medium sherry
4 egg whites, plus
   egg shells

4 ounces cooked chicken, thinly sliced
salt and pepper

1 Place the chicken stock and sherry in a large saucepan and heat gently for 5 minutes.

2 Add the egg whites and the egg shells to the chicken stock and whisk until the mixture begins to boil.

3 Remove the pan from the heat and allow the mixture to subside for 10 minutes. Repeat this process three times. This allows the egg white to trap the sediments in the chicken stock to clarify the soup. Let the consommé cool for 5 minutes.

4 Carefully place a piece of fine cheesecloth over a clean saucepan. Ladle the soup over the cheesecloth and strain into the saucepan.

5 Repeat this process twice, then gently reheat the consommé. Season with salt and pepper to taste, then add the cooked chicken slices. Pour the soup into a warm serving dish or individual bowls.

6 Garnish the consommé with any of the suggestions in the Cook's Tip, right.

COOK'S TIP

Consommé is usually garnished with freshly cooked pasta shapes, noodles, rice, or lightly cooked vegetables. Alternatively, you could garnish it with omelet strips, drained first on paper towels.

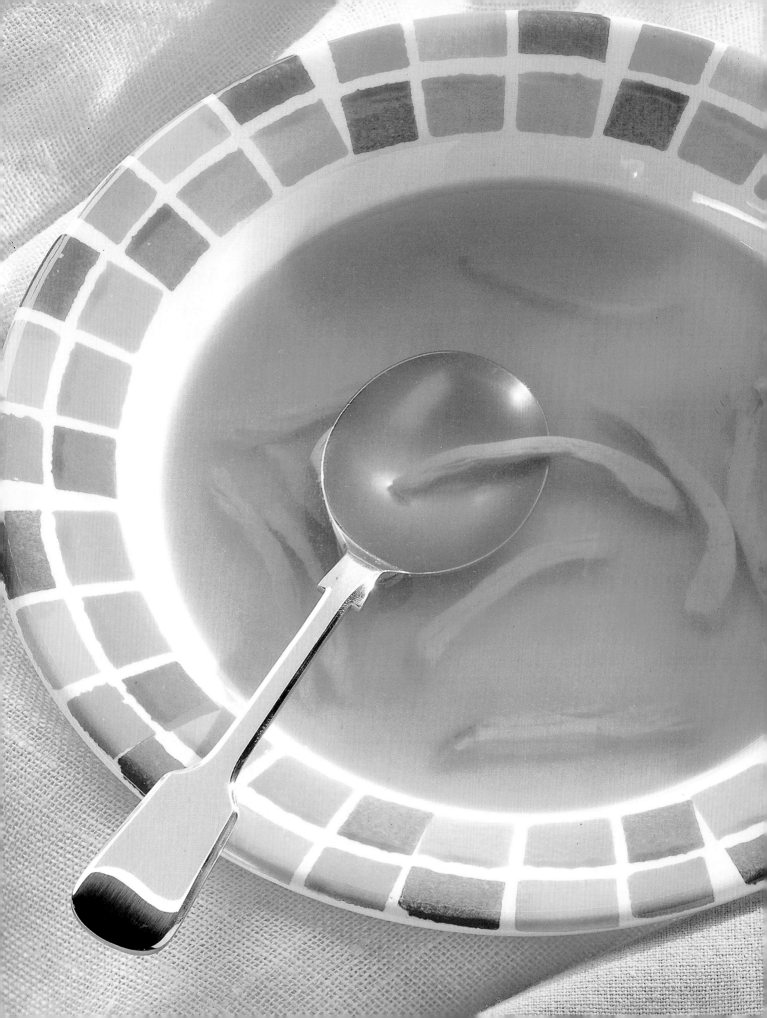

Chicken Mulligatawny Soup

*This spicy soup was brought to the west by British army
and service personnel returning from India.*

Serves 4

INGREDIENTS

4 tablespoons butter
1 onion, sliced
1 garlic clove, crushed
1 pound 2 ounces chicken, diced
1/3 cup smoked bacon, diced
1 small turnip, diced
2 carrots, diced
1 small cooking apple, diced

2 tablespoons mild curry powder
1 tablespoon curry paste
1 tablespoon tomato paste
1 tablespoon all-purpose flour
5 cups chicken stock
2/3 cup heavy cream
salt and pepper

1 teaspoon chopped fresh
   cilantro, to garnish
boiled or fried rice, to serve

1 Melt the butter in a large
  saucepan and cook the onion,
garlic, chicken, and bacon for
5 minutes.

2 Add the turnip, carrots, and
  apple and cook for a further
2 minutes.

3 Blend in the curry powder,
  curry paste, and tomato
paste, and sprinkle over the all-
purpose flour.

4 Add the chicken stock and
  bring to a boil, cover, and
simmer over gentle heat for about
1 hour.

5 Process the soup in a food
  processor until smooth.
Reheat, season well with salt and
pepper to taste, and gradually
blend in the heavy cream. Garnish
the soup with chopped fresh
cilantro and serve over small bowls
of boiled or fried rice.

COOK'S TIP

*This soup may be frozen for
up to 1 month; if stored for any
longer, the spices may cause
it to taste musty.*

Chicken & Pea Soup

A hearty soup that is so simple to make, yet packed with flavor.
You can use either whole green peas or green or yellow split peas.

Serves 4–6

INGREDIENTS

3 smoked bacon slices, chopped
2 pounds chicken, chopped
1 large onion, chopped
1 tablespoon butter
2¹/₂ cups ready-soaked peas
10 cups chicken stock
²/₃ cup heavy cream

2 tablespoons chopped fresh parsley
salt and pepper
cheese croûtes, to garnish

1 Put the bacon, chicken, and onion into a large saucepan with a little butter and cook over gentle heat for 8 minutes.

2 Add the peas and the stock to the pan, bring to a boil, season lightly with salt and pepper, cover, and simmer for 2 hours.

3 Blend the heavy cream into the soup, sprinkle with parsley, and top with cheese croûtes (see Cook's Tip).

COOK'S TIP

Croûtes are slices of French bread that are fried or baked, then they can be sprinkled with grated cheese and lightly toasted.

VARIATION

Use 3¹/₂ ounces chopped ham instead of the bacon, if desired.

COOK'S TIP

If using dried peas, soak them for several hours or overnight in a large bowl of cold water. Alternatively, bring them to a boil in a pan of cold water. Remove from the heat and let cool in the water. Drain and rinse the peas before adding them to the soup.

Cream of Chicken Soup

Tarragon adds a delicate aniseed flavor to this tasty soup.
If you can't find tarragon, use parsley for a fresh taste.

Serves 4

INGREDIENTS

4 tablespoons unsalted butter
1 large onion, peeled and chopped
$10^{1}/_{2}$ ounces cooked chicken,
  shredded finely
$2^{1}/_{2}$ cups chicken stock
1 tablespoon chopped fresh tarragon

$^{2}/_{3}$ cup heavy cream
salt and pepper
fresh tarragon leaves, to garnish
deep fried croûtons, to serve

1 Melt the butter in a large saucepan and fry the onion for 3 minutes.

2 Add the chicken to the saucepan with $1^{1}/_{4}$ cups of the chicken stock.

3 Bring to a boil and simmer for 20 minutes. Let cool, then process until smooth.

4 Add the remainder of the stock and season with salt and pepper.

5 Add the chopped tarragon, pour the soup into a tureen or individual serving bowls, and add a swirl of cream.

6 Garnish the soup with fresh tarragon and serve with deep-fried croûtons.

VARIATION

To make garlic croûtons, crush 3–4 garlic cloves in a pestle and mortar and add to the oil.

VARIATION

If you can't find fresh tarragon, dried tarragon makes an excellent substitute. Light cream can be used instead of the heavy cream.

Chicken Soup with Cilantro Dumplings

Use the strained vegetables and chicken to make little patties. Simply mash with a little butter, shape them into round cakes, and fry in butter or oil until golden brown.

Serves 6-8

INGREDIENTS

2 pounds chicken meat, sliced
1/2 cup all-purpose flour
1/2 cup butter
3 tablespoons sunflower oil
1 large carrot, chopped
1 stalk celery, chopped
1 onion, chopped
1 small turnip, chopped
1/2 cup sherry

1 teaspoon thyme
1 bay leaf
8 cups chicken stock
salt and pepper
crusty bread, to serve

DUMPLINGS:
1/2 cup self-rising flour
1 cup fresh bread crumbs
2 tablespoons shredded suet
2 tablespoons chopped fresh cilantro
2 tablespoons finely grated
  lemon rind
1 egg
salt and pepper

1 Coat the chicken pieces with the flour and season.

2 Melt the butter in a saucepan and fry the chicken pieces until they are lightly browned.

3 Add the oil to the pan and brown the vegetables. Add the sherry and the remaining ingredients, except the stock.

4 Cook for 10 minutes, then add the stock. Simmer for 3 hours, then strain into a clean saucepan, and let cool.

5 To make the dumplings, mix together all the dry ingredients in a large clean bowl. Add the egg and blend in thoroughly, then add enough milk to make a moist dough.

6 Shape into small balls and roll them in a little flour.

7 Cook the dumplings in boiling salted water for 10 minutes.

8 Remove them carefully with a slotted spoon and add them to the soup. Cook for a further 12 minutes, then serve.

Dickensian Chicken Broth

This soup is made with traditional Scottish ingredients. It should be left for at least two days before being reheated, then served with oatmeal cakes or bread.

Serves 4

INGREDIENTS

$^1/_3$ cup pre-soaked dried peas

2 pounds diced chicken,
    fat removed

5 cups chicken stock

$2^1/_2$ cups water

$^1/_4$ cup barley

1 large carrot, peeled and diced

1 small turnip, peeled and diced

1 large leek, thinly sliced

1 red onion, finely chopped

salt and white pepper

1 Put the peas and chicken into a pan, add the stock and water, and bring slowly to a boil.

2 Skim the stock as it boils using a slotted spoon.

3 When all the fat is removed, add the washed barley and salt to taste, and simmer for 35 minutes.

4 Add the remaining ingredients and simmer for 2 hours.

5 Skim the surface of the soup again and allow the broth to stand for at least 24 hours. Reheat, adjust the seasoning, and serve.

VARIATION

This soup is just as delicious made with beef or lamb. Substitute 8 ounces lean sirloin beef or lean lamb fillet for the chicken. Trim any fat from the meat and cut into thin strips before using.

COOK'S TIP

Use either whole grain barley or pearl barley. Only the outer husk is removed from whole grain barley and when cooked, it has a nutty flavor and a chewy texture.

Cream of Chicken & Orange Soup

For a tangy flavor, lemons can be used instead of oranges, or the recipe can be adapted to make duck and orange soup.

Serves 4

INGREDIENTS

4 tablespoons butter
8 shallots, thinly sliced
2 medium carrots, thinly sliced
2 stalks celery,
   thinly sliced

8 ounces skinless chicken breast,
   finely chopped
3 oranges
5 cups chicken stock
$^2/_3$ cup heavy cream
salt and white pepper

sprig of parsley and 3 orange slices,
   to garnish
soda bread, to serve

1 Melt the butter in a large saucepan, add the shallots, carrot, celery, and chicken meat, and cook gently for 8 minutes, stirring occasionally.

2 Using a potato peeler or sharp knife, thinly pare the oranges and blanch the rind in boiling water for about 3 minutes.

3 Squeeze the juice from the oranges. Add the orange rind and orange juice to the pan, together with the chicken stock.

4 Bring slowly to a boil and simmer for 50 minutes. Cool the soup then process in a blender or food processor until smooth.

5 Return the soup to the saucepan, reheat, season to taste, and add the cream. Do not boil at this stage or the soup will curdle.

6 Transfer the soup to a warm tureen or individual bowls. Garnish with a sprig of parsley, orange slices, and serve with soda bread.

VARIATION

Use 2 small lemons in place of the oranges. Look for organic or unwaxed lemons when using rind.

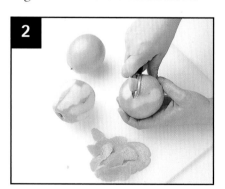

Chicken, Guinea Fowl, & Spaghetti Soup

Guinea fowl, originally from Africa, is extensively farmed in England. It has a similar texture to chicken, and although it has a milder flavor than other game, it has a slightly gamier flavor than chicken.

Serves 6

INGREDIENTS

1 pound 2 ounces skinless chicken, chopped
1 pound 2 ounces skinless guinea fowl meat
2$\frac{1}{2}$ cups chicken stock
1 small onion

6 peppercorns
1 teaspoon cloves
pinch of mace
$\frac{2}{3}$ cup heavy cream
2 teaspoons butter
2 teaspoons all-purpose flour

1 cup quick-cook spaghetti, broken into short lengths and cooked
2 tablespoons chopped fresh parsley, to garnish

1 Put the chicken and guinea fowl meat into a large saucepan with the chicken stock.

2 Bring to a boil and add the onion, peppercorns, cloves, and mace. Simmer gently for about 2 hours, until the stock is reduced by one third.

3 Strain the soup, skim off any fat, and remove any bones from the chicken and guinea fowl.

4 Return the soup and the chicken and guinea fowl meat to a clean saucepan. Add the heavy cream and bring to a boil slowly.

5 To make a roux, melt the butter and stir in the flour until it has a paste-like consistency. Add to the soup, stirring until slightly thickened.

6 Just before serving, add the cooked spaghetti.

7 Transfer the soup to individual serving bowls, garnish with parsley, and serve.

VARIATION

Guinea fowl is available from specialty grocers, but you could use quail or other game bird.

Cream of Chicken & Tomato Soup

This soup is very good made with fresh tomatoes,
but if you prefer, you can use canned tomatoes.

Serves 2

INGREDIENTS

4 tablespoons sweet butter
1 large onion, chopped
1 pound 2 ounces chicken,
  shredded very finely
2^1/$_2$ cups chicken stock
6 medium tomatoes, finely chopped

pinch of baking soda
1 tablespoon sugar
^{2}/$_3$ cup heavy cream
salt and pepper
fresh basil leaves, to garnish
croûtons, to serve

1 Melt the butter in a large
saucepan and fry the onion
and shredded chicken for
5 minutes.

2 Add 1^1/$_4$ cups of the chicken
stock to the pan, together
with the chopped tomatoes and
baking soda.

3 Bring the soup to a boil and
simmer for 20 minutes.

4 Let the soup cool, then
process in a food processor.

5 Add the remaining chicken
stock, season with salt and
pepper, then add the sugar. Pour
the soup into a tureen and add a
swirl of heavy cream. Serve the
soup with croûtons and garnish
with fresh basil leaves.

COOK'S TIP

For a healthier version of this soup,
use light cream instead
of the heavy cream
and omit the sugar.

VARIATION

For an Italian-style soup, add
1 tablespoon chopped fresh basil
with the stock in step 2.
Alternatively, add ^{1}/$_2$ *teaspoon curry*
powder or chile powder to make a
spicier version of this soup.

Chicken Wonton Soup

*This Chinese-style soup is delicious as a starter
to an Asian meal or as a light meal.*

Serves 4-6

INGREDIENTS

FILLING:

12 ounces ground chicken

1 tablespoon soy sauce

1 teaspoon grated, fresh ginger root

1 garlic clove, crushed

2 teaspoons sherry

2 scallions, chopped

1 teaspoon sesame oil

1 egg white

$\frac{1}{2}$ teaspoon cornstarch

$\frac{1}{2}$ teaspoon sugar

about 35 wonton wrappers

SOUP:

6 cups chicken stock

1 tablespoon light soy sauce

1 scallion, shredded

1 small carrot, cut into
very thin slices

1 Combine all the ingredients for the filling and mix well.

2 Place a small spoonful of the filling in the center of each wonton wrapper.

3 Dampen the edges and gather up the wonton wrapper to form a pouch enclosing the filling.

4 Cook the filled wontons in boiling water for 1 minute, or until they float to the top.

5 Remove with a slotted spoon. Bring the chicken stock to a boil.

6 Add the soy sauce, shredded scallion, carrot, and wontons to the soup. Simmer gently for 2 minutes, then serve.

VARIATION

Instead of the chicken, you can use ground pork.

COOK'S TIP

Look for wonton wrappers in Chinese or Asian supermarkets. Fresh wrappers can be found in the chilled compartment and they can be frozen if desired. Wrap them in plastic wrap before freezing.

Chicken & Cheese Potato Skins

Use the breasts from a roasted chicken for this delicious, healthy snack. Served with a mixed salad,
it is an ideal light meal for a summer's day.

Serves 4

INGREDIENTS

4 large baking potatoes
9 ounces cooked, boneless
   chicken breasts
4 scallions

1 cup reduced-fat cream cheese
   or Quark
pepper

coleslaw, salad greens, or a mixed
   salad, to serve

1 Scrub the potatoes and prick them all over with a fork. Bake in a preheated oven at 400°F for about 50 minutes, until tender, or cook in a microwave on High/100% power for 12–15 minutes.

2 Using a sharp knife, dice the chicken, trim and thickly slice the scallions, and mix with the cream cheese or Quark.

3 Cut a cross through the top of each potato and pull slightly apart. Spoon the chicken filling into the potatoes and sprinkle with freshly ground black pepper. Serve immediately with coleslaw, salad greens, or a mixed salad.

VARIATION

For another delicious filling, fry 9 ounces button mushrooms in a little butter. Mix with the chicken, then add ⅔ cup unsweetened yogurt, 1 tablespoon tomato paste, and 2 teaspoons mild curry powder. Blend well and use to fill the potato skins.

COOK'S TIP

Look for Quark in the chilled section. It is a reduced-fat, white, fresh curd cheese made from cow's milk with a delicate, slightly sour flavor.

Sticky Chicken Drumsticks with Mango Salsa

Delicious served hot or cold, and any leftover chicken can be packed in lunchboxes for a tasty alternative to sandwiches.

Serves 4

INGREDIENTS

8 skinless chicken drumsticks
3 tablespoons mango chutney
2 teaspoons Dijon mustard
2 teaspoons oil
1 teaspoon paprika
1 teaspoon black mustard seeds,
   roughly crushed

$1/2$ teaspoon turmeric
2 garlic cloves, chopped
salt and pepper

SALSA:
1 mango, diced
1 tomato, finely chopped

$1/2$ red onion, thinly sliced
2 tablespoons chopped fresh cilantro

1 Using a small, sharp knife, slash each drumstick three or four times then place in a roasting pan.

2 In a small bowl, mix together the mango chutney, mustard, oil, spices, garlic, and salt and pepper and spoon over the chicken drumsticks, turning until they are coated all over with the glaze.

3 Cook in a preheated oven at 400°F for 40 minutes, brushing with the glaze several times during cooking until the chicken is well browned and the juices run clear when pierced with the point of a sharp knife.

4 To make the salsa, combine the mango, tomato, onion, and cilantro. Season to taste and chill until required.

5 Arrange the chicken drumsticks on a serving plate and serve hot or cold with the mango salsa.

VARIATION

Use mild curry powder instead of the turmeric.

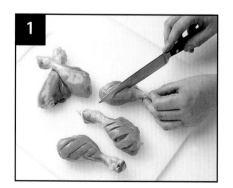

Open Chicken Sandwiches

These tasty sandwiches are good as a snack on their own or they can be served as part of a spread.

Serves 6

INGREDIENTS

6 thick slices of bread or a large
   French loaf cut lengthwise, then
   cut into 6 pieces, and buttered
3 hard-cooked eggs,
   the yolk rubbed through a strainer
   and the white chopped

2 tablespoons butter, softened
2 tablespoons English mustard
1 teaspoon anchovy extract
2 cups grated cheddar cheese
3 cooked, skinless chicken breasts,
   finely chopped
12 slices tomato

12 slices cucumber
pepper

1 Remove the crusts from the bread (optional).

2 Reserve the yolk and the white separately from 1 egg.

3 In a large bowl, mix the remaining egg with the softened butter, English mustard, and anchovy extract and season well with pepper.

4 Mix in the grated cheddar cheese and chicken and spread the mixture on the bread.

5 Make alternate rows of the egg yolk and the egg white over the chicken mixture. Arrange the tomato and cucumber slices over the egg rows and serve.

COOK'S TIP

To soften butter, let it stand at room temperature for 30 minutes or, if you are short of time, cream it in a bowl with a fork. Alternatively, there are now varieties of soft butter available from supermarkets.

COOK'S TIP

If you prefer a less hot flavor, use a milder mustard. Add mayonnaise, if desired, and garnish with watercress.

VARIATION

Add 1¾ ounces finely chopped broiled bacon to the chicken and cheese mixture for a crunchier texture.

Chicken Pepperonata

All the sunshine colors and flavors of the Mediterranean are combined in this easy dish.

Serves 4

INGREDIENTS

8 skinless chicken thighs
2 tablespoons whole
    wheat flour
2 tablespoons olive oil
1 small onion, thinly sliced
1 garlic clove, crushed

1 large red bell pepper, thinly sliced
1 large yellow bell pepper,
    thinly sliced
1 large green bell pepper,
    thinly sliced
14 ounce can chopped tomatoes

1 tablespoon chopped oregano
salt and pepper
fresh oregano, to garnish
crusty whole-wheat bread, to serve

1 Remove and discard the skin from the chicken thighs and toss them in the flour.

2 Heat the oil in a wide skillet and fry the chicken quickly until sealed and lightly browned, then remove from the pan. Add the onion to the pan and gently fry until soft. Add the garlic, bell peppers, tomatoes, and oregano, then bring to a boil, stirring.

3 Arrange the chicken over the vegetables, season well with salt and pepper, then cover tightly, and simmer for 20–25 minutes ,or until the chicken is cooked completely and tender.

4 Season to taste, garnish with oregano, and serve with crusty whole-wheat bread.

COOK'S TIP

If you do not have fresh oregano, use canned tomatoes with herbs already added.

COOK'S TIP

For extra flavor, halve the bell peppers and broil under a preheated broiler until the skins are charred. Let cool, then remove the skins and seeds. Slice the bell peppers thinly and use in the recipe.

Chicken & Herb Fritters

These fritters are delicious served with salad greens,
a fresh vegetable salsa, or a chile sauce dip.

Makes 8

INGREDIENTS

1 pound 2 ounces mashed potato,
  with butter added
1$^{1}/_{3}$ cups chopped,
  cooked chicken
$^{2}/_{3}$ cups cooked ham,
  finely chopped

1 tablespoon mixed herbs
2 eggs, lightly beaten
milk
2 cups fresh brown bread crumbs
oil, for shallow frying
salt and pepper

sprig of fresh parsley, to garnish
salad greens, to serve

1 In a large bowl, blend the potatoes, chicken, ham, herbs, and 1 egg, and season well.

2 Shape the mixture into small balls or flat pancakes.

3 Add a little milk to the second egg.

4 Place the bread crumbs on a plate. Dip the balls in the egg and milk mixture, then roll in the bread crumbs to coat them completely.

5 Heat the cooking oil in a large skillet and cook the fritters until they are golden brown. Garnish with a sprig of fresh parsley and serve at once with salad greens.

COOK'S TIP

A mixture of chopped fresh tarragon and parsley makes a fresh and flavorful addition to these fritters.

COOK'S TIP

To make a piquant tomato sauce to serve with the fritters, heat $^{3}/_{4}$ cup sieved tomatoes and 4 tablespoons dry white wine. Season, remove from the heat, and add 4 tablespoon unsweetened yogurt. Return to the heat and add chile powder to taste.

Oat Chicken Pieces

*A very low-fat chicken recipe with a refreshingly light, mustard-spiced sauce,
which is ideal for a healthy lunchbox or a light meal with salad.*

Serves 4

INGREDIENTS

$1/3$ cup rolled oats
1 tablespoon chopped fresh rosemary
4 skinless chicken quarters
1 egg white
$1/2$ cup ricotta cheese
2 teaspoons wholegrain mustard

salt and pepper
grated carrot salad, to serve

1 Mix together the rolled oats, fresh rosemary, and salt and pepper.

2 Brush each piece of chicken evenly with egg white, then coat in the oat mixture. Place on a cookie sheet and bake in a preheated oven at 400°F for about 40 minutes, or until the juices run clear when the chicken is pierced with the point of a sharp knife.

3 In a bowl, mix together the ricotta cheese and wholegrain mustard, season with salt and pepper to taste, then serve with the chicken, hot or cold, with a grated carrot salad.

VARIATION

To make oat chicken nuggets, chop up 4 skinless, boneless chicken breasts into small pieces. Reduce the cooking time by about 10 minutes and test for doneness. These nuggets would be ideal at a picnic, buffet, or children's party.

VARIATION

Add 1 tablespoon sesame or sunflower seeds to the oat mixture for an even crunchier texture. Experiment with different herbs, instead of the rosemary.

Solomongundy

The rollmops featured in this recipe are fillets of marinated herring wrapped around pickles.
They are available at specialty grocers.

Serves 4

INGREDIENTS

1 large lettuce

4 chicken breasts,
cooked and thinly sliced

8 rollmop herrings and
their marinade

6 hard-cooked eggs, quartered

$^2/_3$ cup sliced cooked ham

$2^2/_3$ cups sliced roast beef

$^2/_3$ cup sliced roast lamb

1 cup snow peas, cooked

$^3/_4$ cup seedless black grapes

20 stuffed olives, sliced

12 shallots, boiled

$^1/_2$ cup slivered almonds

$^1/_3$ cup golden raisins

2 oranges

sprig of mint

salt and pepper

fresh crusty bread, to serve

1 Spread out the lettuce leaves to cover a large oval platter.

2 Arrange the chicken in three sections on the platter.

3 Place the rollmops, eggs, and meats in lines or sections over the remainder of the platter.

4 Use the snow peas, grapes, olives, shallots, almonds, and golden raisins to fill in the spaces between the lines or sections.

5 Grate the rind from the oranges and sprinkle it over the whole platter. Peel and slice the oranges and add the orange slices and mint sprig to the platter. Season to taste with salt and pepper. Sprinkle with the rollmop herring marinade and serve.

VARIATION

Should you wish,
serve the Solomongundy with
cold, cooked vegetables, such
as sliced beans, baby corn,
and cooked beets.

Chicken Pan Bagna

Perfect for a picnic or lunchbox, this Mediterranean-style sandwich can be prepared ahead.

Serves 6

INGREDIENTS

1 long French loaf
1 garlic clove
1/2 cup olive oil
3/4 oz can anchovy fillets

12 ounces cold roast chicken
2 large tomatoes, sliced
8 large, pitted black olives, chopped
pepper

1 Using a sharp bread knife, cut the French bread in half lengthwise and open out.

2 Cut the garlic clove in half and rub over the bread.

3 Sprinkle the cut surface of the bread with the olive oil.

4 Drain the anchovies and set aside.

5 Thinly slice the chicken and arrange on top of the bread with the sliced tomatoes and drained anchovies.

6 Scatter with the chopped black olives and plenty of black pepper. Sandwich the loaf back together and wrap tightly in foil until required. Cut into slices to serve.

VARIATION

Instead of putting sliced tomatoes in the sandwich you could rub half a tomato over the cut surface of the bread, squeezing out all the pulp and discarding the skin. Then sprinkle with the olive oil.

COOK'S TIP

Arrange a few fresh basil leaves in between the tomato slices to add a warm, spicy flavor. Use a good quality olive oil in this recipe for extra flavor.

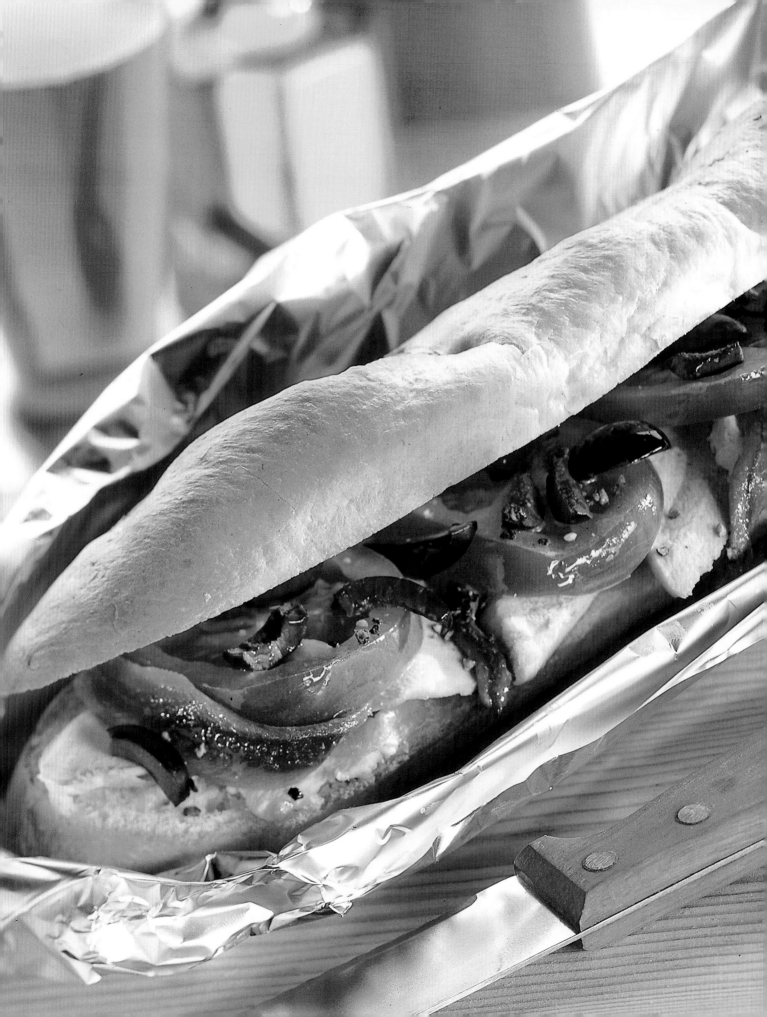

Coronation Chicken

This classic salad is good as a starter or as part of a buffet.
Mango chutney makes a tasty addition.

Serves 6

INGREDIENTS

4 tablespoons olive oil
2 pounds chicken meat, diced
$^2/_3$ cup smoked bacon, diced
12 shallots
2 garlic cloves, crushed
1 tablespoon mild curry powder

$1^1/_4$ cups mayonnaise
1 tablespoon honey
1 tablespoon chopped fresh parsley
$^1/_2$ cup seedless black
  grapes, quartered
pepper

cold saffron rice, to serve

1 Heat the oil in a large skillet and add the chicken, bacon, shallots, garlic, and curry powder. Cook over low heat for about 15 minutes.

2 Spoon the mixture into a clean mixing bowl.

3 Let the mixture cool completely, then season with pepper to taste.

4 Blend the mayonnaise with a little honey, then add the chopped fresh parsley. Toss the chicken in the mixture.

5 Place the mixture in a deep serving dish, garnish with the grapes, and serve with cold saffron rice.

COOK'S TIP

You can use this recipe to fill a potato skin or as a sandwich filling, but cut the chicken into smaller pieces.

VARIATION

Add 2 tablespoons chopped fresh apricots and 2 tablespoons slivered almonds to the sauce in step 4. For a healthier version of this dish, replace the mayonnaise with the same quantity of unsweetened yogurt and omit the honey, otherwise the sauce will be too runny.

Potted Smoked Chicken

This recipe can be made a few days ahead and kept chilled until needed. A food processor makes light work of blending the ingredients, but you can pound by hand for a coarser mixture.

Serves 4–6

INGREDIENTS

2¹/₂ cups chopped smoked chicken
pinch of grated nutmeg
pinch of ground mace
¹/₂ cup butter, softened

2 tablespoons port
2 tablespoons heavy cream
salt and pepper
sprig of fresh parsley, to garnish

brown bread slices and fresh butter,
to serve

1 Place the smoked chicken in a large bowl with the remaining ingredients, and season with salt and pepper to taste.

2 Pound until the mixture is very smooth or process in a food processor.

3 Transfer the mixture to individual earthenware pots or one large pot.

4 Cover each pot with buttered baking parchment and weigh down with cans or weights. Chill in the refrigerator for 4 hours.

5 Remove the parchment and cover with clarified butter (see Cook's Tip).

6 Garnish with a sprig of parsley and serve with slices of brown bread and fresh butter.

COOK'S TIP

The Potted Smoked Chicken can be kept in the refrigerator for 2–3 days, but no longer, as it does not contain any preservatives. It may be stored in the freezer for a maximum of 1 month.

COOK'S TIP

To make clarified butter: place 1 cup butter in a saucepan and heat gently, skimming off the foam as the butter heats—the sediment will sink to the bottom of the pan. When the butter has completely melted, remove the pan from the heat and let stand for at least 4 minutes. Strain the butter through a piece of cheesecloth into a bowl. Let the butter cool a little before pouring it over the surface of the potted chicken.

Cheese Garlic Drumsticks

Ideal for informal parties, these tasty chicken drumsticks can be prepared for cooking a day in advance. Instead of baking the chicken drumsticks, you could cook them on the barbecue instead.

Serves 6

INGREDIENTS

1 tablespoon butter
1 garlic clove, crushed
3 tablespoons chopped fresh parsley
1/2 cup ricotta cheese

4 tablespoons grated Parmesan cheese
3 tablespoons fresh bread crumbs
12 chicken drumsticks
salt and pepper

lemon slices, to garnish

1 Melt the butter in a pan. Add the garlic and fry gently without browning, stirring for 1 minute.

2 Remove the pan from the heat and stir in the parsley, the cheeses, bread crumbs, and seasoning.

3 Carefully loosen the skin around the chicken drumsticks.

4 Using a teaspoon, push about 1 tablespoon of the stuffing under the skin of each drumstick. Arrange the drumsticks in a large roasting pan.

5 Bake in a preheated oven at 375°F for about 45 minutes. Serve hot or cold, garnished with lemon slices.

COOK'S TIP

Any strongly flavored cheese can be used instead of the Parmesan. Try a sharp Cheddar cheese or use another Italian cheese, such as pecorino.

COOK'S TIP

Freshly grated Parmesan has more "bite" than ready-packed grated Parmesan from supermarkets. Grate only as much as you need and wrap the rest in foil—it will then keep for several months in the refrigerator.

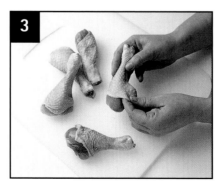

Chicken Rarebit

A tasty dish that can be served alone as a snack or to accompany a light, clear soup.

Serves 4

INGREDIENTS

2 cups grated cheddar cheese, such
  as Wensleydale
1$\frac{1}{3}$ cups shredded,
  cooked chicken
1 tablespoon butter
1 tablespoon Worcestershire sauce

1 teaspoon English mustard powder
2 teaspoons all-purpose flour
4 tablespoons mild beer
4 slices of bread
salt and pepper

1 tablespoon chopped fresh parsley,
  to garnish
cherry tomatoes, to serve

1 Place the grated cheddar cheese, shredded chicken, butter, Worcestershire sauce, mustard powder, all-purpose flour and beer in a small saucepan. Mix all the ingredients together then season with salt and pepper to taste.

2 Gently bring the mixture to a boil, then remove from the heat immediately.

3 Using a wooden spoon, beat until the mixture becomes creamy in texture. Set the mixture aside to cool.

4 Once the chicken mixture has cooled, toast the bread on both sides and spread with the chicken mixture.

5 Place under a preheated broiler until bubbling and golden brown.

6 Sprinkle with a little chopped parsley and serve at once with cherry tomatoes.

COOK'S TIP

This is a variation of Welsh rarebit, which does not traditionally contain chicken. Welsh rarebit topped with a poached egg is called Buck Rarebit.

Waldorf Summer Chicken Salad

This colorful and healthy dish is a variation of a classic salad. Served with crusty brown rolls, it is an ideal light meal for a summer's day

Serves 4

INGREDIENTS

1 pound 2 ounces red apples, diced
3 tablespoons fresh lemon juice
²/₃ cup light mayonnaise
1 head of celery
4 shallots, sliced
1 garlic clove, crushed

³/₄ cup walnuts, chopped
1 pound 2 ounces cooked
  chicken, cubed
1 romaine lettuce

pepper
sliced apple and walnuts, to garnish

1 Place the apples in a bowl with the lemon juice and 1 tablespoon of the mayonnaise. Set aside for 40 minutes.

2 Using a sharp knife, slice the celery very thinly.

3 Add the celery, shallots, garlic, and walnuts to the apple and mix together.

4 Stir in the remaining mayonnaise and blend thoroughly.

5 Add the cooked chicken to the bowl and mix well.

6 Line a glass salad bowl or serving dish with the lettuce leaves. Pile the chicken salad into the center, sprinkle with pepper, and garnish with the apple slices and walnuts.

COOK'S TIP

Soaking the apples in lemon juice prevents discoloration.

COOK'S TIP

Instead of the shallots, use scallions for a milder flavor. Trim the scallions and slice finely.

Old English Spicy Chicken Salad

For this simple, refreshing summer salad you can use leftover roast chicken, or ready-roasted chicken to save time. Add the dressing just before serving, or the spinach will lose its crispness.

Serves 4

INGREDIENTS

9 ounces young spinach leaves
3 stalks celery, thinly sliced
1/2 cucumber
2 scallions
3 tablespoons chopped fresh parsley
12 ounces boneless, roast chicken,
   thinly sliced

DRESSING:
1-inch piece fresh ginger
   root, finely grated
3 tablespoons olive oil
1 tablespoon white wine vinegar
1 tablespoon honey
1/2 teaspoon ground cinnamon
salt and pepper

smoked almonds,
   to garnish (optional)

---

1 Thoroughly wash the spinach leaves, then pat dry with paper towels.

2 Using a sharp knife, thinly slice the celery, cucumber, and scallions. Toss in a large bowl, together with the spinach leaves and parsley.

3 Transfer to serving plates and arrange the chicken over the salad.

4 In a screw-topped jar, combine all the dressing ingredients and shake well to mix.

5 Season to taste, then pour onto the salad. Sprinkle with a few smoked almonds, if using.

VARIATION

Substitute corn salad for the spinach, if desired.

VARIATION

Fresh young spinach leaves go particularly well with fruit—try adding a few fresh raspberries or nectarine slices to make an even more refreshing salad.

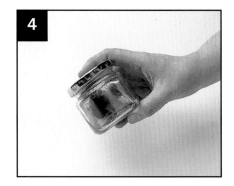

Breast of Chicken with Pear
& Blue Cheese Salad

*The sweetness of the pears complements perfectly the sharp taste of the blue cheese
in this delicious warm salad.*

Serves 6

INGREDIENTS

$^1/_4$ cup olive oil
6 shallots, sliced
1 garlic clove, crushed
2 tablespoons chopped
   fresh tarragon
1 tablespoon English mustard
6 skinless, boneless chicken breasts
1 tablespoon all-purpose flour

$^2/_3$ cup chicken stock
1 apple, finely diced
1 tablespoon chopped walnuts
2 tablespoons heavy cream
salt and pepper

SALAD:
3$^1/_2$ cups cooked rice

2 large pears, diced
1 cup diced blue cheese
1 red bell pepper, diced
1 tablespoon chopped fresh cilantro
1 tablespoon sesame oil

1 Place the olive oil, shallots,
garlic, tarragon, and mustard
in a deep bowl. Season well with
salt and pepper and mix the
ingredients together thoroughly.

2 Place the chicken in the
marinade to coat completely,
cover with plastic wrap, and
chill in the refrigerator for about
4 hours.

3 Drain the chicken, reserving
the marinade. Quickly fry the
chicken in a large, deep nonstick
skillet for 4 minutes on both sides.
Transfer the chicken to a warm
serving dish.

4 Add the marinade to the pan,
bring to a boil, and sprinkle
with the flour. Add the chicken
stock, apple, and walnuts and

gently simmer for 5 minutes.
Return the chicken to the sauce,
add the heavy cream, and cook for
2 minutes.

5 Mix the salad ingredients
together, place a little on each
plate, and top with a chicken breast
and a spoonful of the sauce.

Quick Dishes

One of the marvelous qualities of chicken is that when cut into small pieces, it can be cooked very quickly, which is welcome for those of us who are too busy to spend a lot of time preparing meals. In this section, you can select a tasty, nutritious dish that won't take hours to make. Pasta makes a perfect partner for chicken as it is also quick to cook—Italian Chicken Spirals look impressive and will fool guests into thinking that you have spent hours slaving away in the kitchen. Chicken breasts are cooked with a delicious basil, hazelnut, and garlic filling and then served on a bed of pasta, olives, and sun-dried tomatoes. Smaller cuts of chicken are also ideal for stir-fries that can be quickly cooked to produce tender, moist, and flavorful chicken. Speedy Peanut Pan-fry is a crunchy stir-fry that is served with noodles. Risottos are also an excellent choice for when you are in a hurry—this chapter contains two risotto recipes, although the variations for risotto are endless!

Harlequin Chicken

This colorful, simple dish will tempt the appetites of all the family—it is ideal for toddlers, who enjoy the fun shapes of the multicolored bell peppers.

Serves 4

INGREDIENTS

10 skinless, boneless chicken thighs
1 medium onion
1 medium red bell pepper
1 medium green bell pepper
1 medium yellow bell pepper

1 tablespoon sunflower oil
14 ounce can chopped tomatoes
2 tablespoons chopped fresh parsley
pepper

whole-wheat bread and salad greens,
  to serve

1 Using a sharp knife, cut the chicken thighs into bite-size pieces.

2 Peel and thinly slice the onion. Halve and seed the bell peppers, and cut into small diamond shapes.

3 Heat the oil in a shallow skillet. Add the chicken and onion and fry quickly until golden brown.

4 Add the bell peppers, cook for 2–3 minutes, then stir in the tomatoes and parsley, and season with pepper.

5 Cover tightly and simmer for about 15 minutes, until the chicken and vegetables are tender. Serve hot with whole-wheat bread and salad greens.

COOK'S TIP

You can use dried parsley instead of fresh, but remember that you only need about one half of dried to fresh.

COOK'S TIP

If you are making this dish for young children, the chicken can be finely chopped or ground first.

Steamed Chicken & Spring Vegetable Pockets

A healthy recipe with a delicate Chinese flavor, ideal for tender young summer vegetables. You'll need large spinach leaves to wrap around the chicken, but make sure they are young leaves.

Serves 4

INGREDIENTS

4 boneless, skinless
   chicken breasts
1 teaspoon ground lemon grass
2 scallions, finely chopped
1 cup young carrots
1³/4 cups young zucchini

2 stalks celery
1 teaspoon light soy sauce
³/4 cup spinach leaves
2 teaspoons sesame oil
salt and pepper

1 With a sharp knife, make a slit through one side of each chicken breast to open out a large pocket. Sprinkle the inside of the pocket with lemon grass, salt, and pepper. Tuck the scallions into the pockets.

2 Trim the carrots, zucchini, and celery, then cut into small matchsticks. Plunge them into a pan of boiling water for 1 minute, drain, and toss in the soy sauce.

3 Pack the vegetables into the pockets in each chicken breast and fold over firmly to enclose. Reserve any remaining vegetables. Wash the spinach leaves thoroughly, then drain, and pat dry with paper towels. Wrap the chicken breasts firmly in the spinach leaves to enclose completely. If the leaves are too firm to wrap the chicken easily, steam them for a few seconds, until they are softened and flexible.

4 Place the wrapped chicken in a steamer and steam over rapidly boiling water for 20–25 minutes, depending on size.

5 Stir-fry any leftover vegetable sticks and spinach for 1–2 minutes in the sesame oil and serve with the chicken.

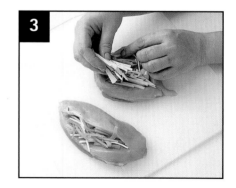

Chicken with Two Bell Pepper Sauce

This quick and simple dish is colorful and healthy.
It would be perfect for an impromptu lunch or supper dish.

Serves 4

INGREDIENTS

2 tablespoons olive oil
2 medium onions, finely chopped
2 garlic cloves, crushed
2 red bell peppers, chopped
good pinch cayenne pepper
2 teaspoons tomato paste

2 yellow bell peppers, chopped
pinch of dried basil
4 skinless, boneless
  chicken breasts
$^2/_3$ cup dry white wine
$^2/_3$ cup chicken stock

bouquet garni
salt and pepper
fresh herbs, to garnish

1 Heat 1 tablespoon of the olive oil in each of two medium saucepans. Place half the chopped onions, 1 of the garlic cloves, the red bell peppers, the cayenne pepper, and the tomato paste in one of the saucepans. Place the remaining chopped onion, garlic, yellow bell peppers and basil in the other pan.

2 Cover each pan and cook over very low heat for 1 hour, until the bell peppers are very soft. If either mixture becomes dry, add a little water. Work each separately in a food processor, then strain separately.

3 Return the sauces separately to each pan and season. The two sauces can be reheated while the chicken is cooking.

4 Put the chicken breasts into a skillet and add the wine and stock. Add the bouquet garni and bring the liquid to a simmer. Cook the chicken for about 20 minutes, until tender.

5 To serve, pour a pool of each sauce onto four serving plates, slice the chicken breasts, and arrange on the plates. Garnish with fresh herbs.

COOK'S TIP

Make your own bouquet garni by tying together sprigs of your favorite herbs with string, or wrap up dried herbs in a piece of cheesecloth. A popular combination is thyme, parsley, and bay.

Chicken Risotto alla Milanese

This is famous throughout the world, and it is perhaps the best known of all Italian risottos, although there are many variations. Risotto rice is also known as arborio rice. It is available at specialty grocers.

Serves 4

INGREDIENTS

¹/₂ cup butter
2 pounds chicken meat, thinly sliced
1 large onion, chopped
2¹/₂ cups risotto rice
2¹/₂ cups chicken stock

²/₃ cup white wine
1 teaspoon crumbled saffron
salt and pepper
¹/₂ cup grated Parmesan cheese,
  to serve

1 Heat 4 tablespoons of the butter in a deep skillet, and fry the chicken and onion until golden brown.

2 Add the rice, stir well, and cook for 15 minutes.

3 Heat the stock until boiling and gradually add to the rice. Add the white wine, saffron, and salt and pepper to taste and mix well. Simmer over low heat for 20 minutes, stirring occasionally, and adding more stock if the risotto becomes too dry.

4 Let stand for a few minutes and just before serving, add a little more stock and simmer for a further 10 minutes. Serve the risotto, sprinkled with the grated Parmesan cheese and the remaining butter.

COOK'S TIP

A risotto should have moist, but separate grains. Stock should be added a little at a time and only when the last addition has been completely absorbed.

VARIATION

The possibilities for risotto are almost endless—try adding any of the following just at the end of cooking time: cashews and corn, lightly sautéed zucchini and basil, or artichokes and oyster mushrooms.

Elizabethan Chicken

*Chicken is surprisingly delicious when combined
with fruits, such as grapes or gooseberries.*

Serves 4

INGREDIENTS

1 tablespoon butter

1 tablespoon sunflower oil

4 skinless, boneless
chicken breasts

4 shallots, finely chopped

$^2/_3$ cup chicken stock

1 tablespoon cider vinegar

1 cup halved seedless grapes

$^1/_2$ cup heavy cream

1 teaspoon freshly grated nutmeg

cornstarch, to thicken, (optional)

salt and pepper

---

1 Heat the butter and sunflower oil in a wide, flameproof casserole or skillet and quickly fry the chicken breasts until golden brown, turning once. Remove the chicken breasts and keep warm while you are cooking the shallots.

2 Add the chopped shallots to the casserole or skillet and fry gently until softened and lightly browned. Return the chicken breasts to the pan.

3 Add the chicken stock and cider vinegar to the pan, bring to a boil, then cover, and simmer gently for 10–12 minutes, stirring occasionally.

4 Transfer the chicken to a serving dish. Add the grapes, cream, and nutmeg to the pan. Heat through, seasoning with salt and pepper to taste. Add a little cornstarch to thicken the sauce, if desired. Pour the sauce over the chicken and serve.

VARIATION

If desired, add a little dry white wine or vermouth to the sauce in step 3.

Speedy Peanut Pan-fry

A complete main course cooked within ten minutes. Thread egg noodles are the ideal accompaniment because they can be cooked quickly and easily while the stir-fry sizzles.

Serves 4

INGREDIENTS

2 cups zucchini
1¹/₃ cups baby corn
3³/₄ cups button mushrooms
3 cups thread
  egg noodles
2 tablespoons corn oil
1 tablespoon sesame oil

8 boneless chicken thighs
  or 4 breasts, thinly sliced
1¹/₂ cups bean sprouts
4 tablespoons smooth
  peanut butter
2 tablespoons soy sauce
2 tablespoons lime or lemon juice
¹/₂ cup roasted peanuts

pepper
cilantro, to garnish

1 Using a sharp knife, trim and thinly slice the zucchini, baby corn, and button mushrooms.

2 Bring a large pan of lightly salted water to a boil and cook the noodles for 3–4 minutes. Meanwhile, heat together the corn oil and sesame oil in a large skillet or wok. Add the chicken and fry over fairly high heat for 1 minute.

3 Add the sliced zucchini, baby corn, and button mushrooms and stir-fry for 5 minutes.

4 Add the bean sprouts, peanut butter, soy sauce, lime or lemon juice, and pepper, then cook for a further 2 minutes.

5 Drain the noodles, transfer to a serving dish, and scatter with the peanuts. Serve with the stir-fried chicken and vegetables, garnished with a sprig of fresh cilantro.

COOK'S TIP

Try serving this stir-fry with rice sticks. These are broad, pale, translucent ribbon noodles made from ground rice.

Prosciutto-wrapped Chicken Cushions

Stuffed with creamy ricotta, nutmeg, and spinach, then wrapped with wafer-thin slices of prosciutto, and gently cooked in white wine.

Serves 4

INGREDIENTS

$^1/_2$ cup frozen spinach, thawed

$^1/_2$ cup ricotta cheese

pinch grated nutmeg

4 skinless, boneless chicken breasts, each weighing 6 ounces

4 slices prosciutto

2 tablespoons butter

1 tablespoon olive oil

12 small onions or shallots

$1^1/_2$ cups button mushrooms, sliced

1 tablespoon all-purpose flour

$^2/_3$ cup dry white or red wine

$1^1/_4$ cups chicken stock

salt and pepper

carrot purée and green beans, to serve

1 Put the spinach into a strainer and press out the water with a spoon. Mix with the ricotta and nutmeg and season with salt and pepper to taste.

2 Using a sharp knife, slit each chicken breast through the side and enlarge each cut to form a pocket. Fill with the spinach mixture, reshape the chicken breasts, wrap each breast tightly in a slice of ham, and secure with toothpicks. Cover and chill in the refrigerator.

3 Heat the butter and oil in a skillet and brown the chicken breasts for 2 minutes on each side. Transfer the chicken to a large, shallow ovenproof dish and keep warm until required.

4 Fry the onions and mushrooms for 2–3 minutes, until lightly browned. Stir in the all-purpose flour, then gradually add the wine and stock. Bring to a boil, stirring constantly. Season to taste and spoon the mixture around the chicken.

5 Cook the chicken, uncovered, in a preheated oven at 400°F for 20 minutes. Turn the breasts over and cook for a further 10 minutes. Remove the toothpicks and serve with the sauce, together with carrot purée and green beans, if desired.

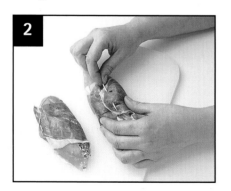

Poached Breast of Chicken with Whiskey Sauce

After cooking with stock and vegetables, chicken breasts are served with a velvety sauce made from whiskey and crème fraîche.

Serves 6

INGREDIENTS

2 tablespoons butter
1/2 cup shredded leeks
1/3 cup diced carrot
1/4 cup diced celery
4 shallots, sliced

2 1/2 cups chicken stock
6 chicken breasts
1/4 cup whiskey
1 scant cup crème fraîche or
   sour cream

2 tablespoons freshly grated horseradish
1 teaspoon honey, warmed
1 teaspoon chopped fresh parsley
salt and pepper
sprig of fresh parsley, to garnish

1 Melt the butter in a large saucepan and add the leeks, carrot, celery, and shallots. Cook for 3 minutes, add half the chicken stock, and cook for about 8 minutes.

2 Add the remaining chicken stock, bring to a boil, add the chicken breasts, and cook for 10 minutes.

3 Remove the chicken and thinly slice. Place on a large, hot serving dish and keep warm until required.

4 In another saucepan, heat the whiskey until reduced by half. Strain the chicken stock through a fine strainer, add to the pan, and reduce the liquid by half.

5 Add the crème fraîche or sour cream, the horseradish and the honey. Heat gently and add the chopped parsley and salt and pepper to taste. Stir well.

6 Pour a little of the whiskey sauce around the chicken and pour the remaining sauce into a sauceboat to serve.

7 Serve with a vegetable patty made from the leftover vegetables, mashed potato, and fresh vegetables. Garnish with the parsley sprig.

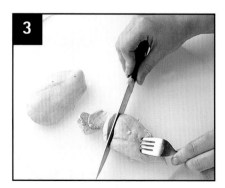

Deviled Chicken

Chicken is spiked with cayenne pepper and paprika and finished off with a fruity sauce.

Serves 2–3

INGREDIENTS

1/4 cup all-purpose flour

1 tablespoon cayenne pepper

1 teaspoon paprika

12 ounces skinless, boneless
  chicken, diced

2 tablespoons butter

1 onion, finely chopped

scant 2 cups milk, warmed

4 tablespoons apple purée

3/4 cup white grapes

2/3 cup sour cream

sprinkle of paprika, to garnish

1 Mix the flour, cayenne pepper, and paprika together and use to coat the chicken.

2 Shake off any excess flour. Melt the butter in a saucepan and gently fry the chicken with the onion for 4 minutes.

3 Stir in the flour and spice mixture. Add the milk slowly, stirring until the sauce thickens.

4 Simmer until the sauce is smooth.

5 Add the apple purée and grapes and simmer gently for 20 minutes.

6 Transfer the chicken and deviled sauce to a serving dish and top with sour cream and a sprinkle of paprika.

VARIATION

For a healthier alternative to the sour cream in this recipe, use unsweetened yogurt.

COOK'S TIP

Add more paprika if desired—as it is quite a mild spice, you can add plenty without its being too overpowering.

Italian Chicken Spirals

Steaming allows you to cook without fat, and these little foil packets retain all the natural juices of the chicken while cooking conveniently over the pasta as it boils.

Serves 4

INGREDIENTS

4 skinless, boneless, chicken breasts
1 cup fresh basil leaves
2 tablespoons hazelnuts
1 garlic clove, crushed
2 cups whole wheat
   pasta spirals

2 sun-dried tomatoes
   or fresh tomatoes
1 tablespoon lemon juice
1 tablespoon olive oil
1 tablespoon capers
$1/2$ cup black olives

salt and pepper

1 Beat the chicken breasts with a rolling pin to flatten evenly.

2 Place the basil and hazelnuts in a food processor and process until finely chopped. Mix with the garlic, salt, and pepper.

3 Spread the basil mixture over the chicken breasts and roll up from one short end to enclose the filling. Wrap the chicken rolls tightly in foil so that they hold their shape, then seal the ends well.

4 Bring a large pan of lightly salted water to a boil and cook the pasta until tender, but still firm to the bite.

5 Place the chicken parcels in a steamer basket or colander set over the pan, cover tightly, and steam for 10 minutes. Meanwhile, dice the tomatoes.

6 Drain the pasta and return to the pan with the lemon juice, olive oil, tomatoes, capers, and olives. Heat through.

7 Pierce the chicken with a sharp knife to make sure that the juices run clear and not pink, then slice the chicken, arrange it over the pasta, and serve.

VARIATION

Sun-dried tomatoes have a wonderful, rich flavor, but if you can't find them, use fresh tomatoes.

Garlic Chicken Cushions

Stuffed with creamy ricotta, spinach, and garlic, then gently cooked in a rich tomato sauce, this is a suitable dish to make ahead of time.

Serves 4

INGREDIENTS

4 partially-boned chicken breasts
$^1/_2$ cup frozen spinach, thawed
$^1/_2$ cup ricotta cheese
2 garlic cloves, crushed
1 tablespoon olive oil
1 onion, chopped

1 red bell pepper, sliced
14 ounce can chopped tomatoes
6 tablespoons wine or chicken stock
10 stuffed olives, sliced

salt and pepper
pasta, to serve

1 Make a slit between the skin and meat on one side of each chicken breast. Lift the skin to form a pocket, being careful to leave the skin attached to the other side.

2 Put the spinach into a strainer and press out the water with a spoon. Mix with the ricotta, half the garlic, and seasoning.

3 Spoon the spinach and ricotta mixture under the skin of each chicken breast, then secure the edge of the skin with toothpicks.

4 Heat the oil in a skillet, add the onion, and fry for a minute, stirring. Add the remaining garlic and red bell pepper and cook for 2 minutes. Stir in the tomatoes, wine or stock, olives, and seasoning. Set the sauce aside and chill the chicken if preparing in advance.

5 Bring the sauce to a boil, pour into a shallow ovenproof dish, and arrange the chicken breasts on top in a single layer.

6 Cook, uncovered, in a preheated oven at 400°F for 35 minutes, until the chicken is golden and cooked through. Test by making a slit in one of the chicken breasts with a sharp knife to make sure the juices run clear and not pink. Spoon a little of the sauce over the chicken breasts then transfer to warm individual serving plates. Serve with pasta.

Chicken Strips & Dips

Very simple to make and easy to eat with fingers, this dish can be served warm for a light lunch or cold as part of a buffet.

Serves 2

INGREDIENTS

2 boneless chicken breasts
2 tablespoons all-purpose flour
1 tablespoon sunflower oil

PEANUT DIP:
3 tablespoons smooth or crunchy
  peanut butter
4 tablespoons unsweetened yogurt
1 teaspoon grated orange rind
orange juice (optional)

TOMATO DIP:
5 tablespoons ricotta cheese
1 medium tomato
2 teaspoons tomato paste
1 teaspoon chopped fresh chives

1 Using a sharp knife, slice the chicken into fairly thin strips and toss in the flour to coat.

2 Heat the oil in a nonstick skillet and fry the chicken until golden and thoroughly cooked. Remove the chicken strips from the pan and drain well on absorbent paper towels.

3 To make the peanut dip, mix together all the ingredients in a bowl (if desired, add a little orange juice to thin the dip).

4 To make the tomato dip, chop the tomato and mix with the remaining ingredients.

5 Serve the chicken strips with the dips and a selection of vegetable sticks for dipping.

VARIATION

For a lower-fat alternative, poach the strips of chicken in a small amount of boiling chicken stock for 6–8 minutes.

VARIATION

For a refreshing guacamole dip, combine 1 mashed avocado, 2 finely chopped scallions, 1 chopped tomato, 1 crushed garlic clove, and a squeeze of lemon juice. Remember to add the lemon juice immediately after the avocado has been mashed to prevent discoloration.

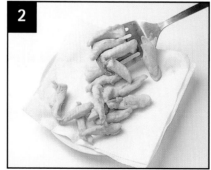

Chicken Lady Jayne

This dish has a surprising combination of coffee and brandy flavors—it works very well!

Serves 4

INGREDIENTS

4 chicken breasts, each about
    4^{1}/$_{2}$ ounces
4 tablespoons corn oil
8 shallots, sliced
rind and juice of 1 lemon

2 teaspoons Worcestershire sauce
4 tablespoons chicken stock
1 tablespoon chopped fresh parsley
3 tablespoons coffee liqueur
3 tablespoons brandy, warmed

1 Place the chicken breasts on a chopping board, cover with plastic wrap and pound them until evenly flattened with a wooden meat mallet or a rolling pin.

2 Heat the oil in a large skillet and fry the chicken for 3 minutes on each side. Add the shallots and cook for a further 3 minutes.

3 Sprinkle with lemon juice and lemon rind and add the Worcestershire sauce and chicken stock. Cook for 2 minutes, then sprinkle with the chopped fresh parsley.

4 Add the coffee liqueur and the brandy and flame the chicken by lighting the spirit with a taper or long match. Cook until the flame is extinguished and serve.

COOK'S TIP

Flattening the breasts means that they take less time to cook.

COOK'S TIP

Instead of chicken breasts, suprêmes can also be used. A suprême is a chicken fillet that sometimes has part of the wing bone remaining.

Golden Glazed Chicken

A glossy glaze with sweet and fruity flavors coats chicken breasts in this tasty recipe.

Serves 6

INGREDIENTS

6 boneless chicken breasts
1 teaspoon turmeric
1 tablespoon wholegrain mustard
1¼ cups orange juice
2 tablespoons clear honey
2 tablespoons sunflower oil

1³/₄ cups long grain rice
1 orange
3 tablespoons chopped mint
salt and pepper
mint sprigs, to garnish

1 With a sharp knife, mark the surface of the chicken breasts in a diamond pattern. Mix together the turmeric, mustard, orange juice, and honey and pour over the chicken. Chill until required.

2 Lift the chicken from the marinade and pat dry on paper towels.

3 Heat the oil in a wide pan, add the chicken, and sauté until golden, turning once. Drain off any excess oil. Pour the marinade over it, cover, and simmer for 10–15 minutes, until the chicken is tender.

4 Boil the rice in lightly salted water until tender, and drain well. Finely grate the rind from the orange and stir it into the rice with the mint.

5 Using a sharp knife, remove the peel and white pith from the orange and cut the flesh into segments.

6 Serve the chicken with the orange and mint rice, garnished with orange segments and mint sprigs.

VARIATION

To make a slightly sharper sauce, use small grapefruit instead of the oranges.

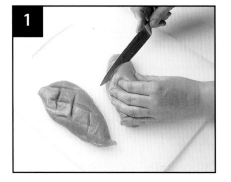

Mediterranean Chicken Packets

This method of cooking makes the chicken aromatic and succulent. It also reduces the amount of oil needed, since the chicken and vegetables cook in their own juices.

Serves 6

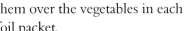

INGREDIENTS

1 tablespoon olive oil
6 skinless chicken breast fillets
2 cups Mozzarella cheese
3¹/₂ cups sliced zucchini
6 large tomatoes, sliced

1 small bunch fresh basil or oregano
pepper
rice or pasta, to serve

1 Cut six pieces of foil each about 10 inches square. Brush the foil squares lightly with oil and set aside until required.

2 With a sharp knife, slash each chicken breast at intervals, then slice the Mozzarella cheese and place between the cuts in the chicken.

3 Divide the zucchini and tomatoes between the pieces of foil and sprinkle with black pepper. Tear or roughly chop the basil or oregano leaves and scatter

them over the vegetables in each foil packet.

4 Place the chicken on top of each pile of vegetables, then wrap in the foil to enclose the chicken and vegetables, tucking in the ends.

5 Place the foil packets on a cookie sheet and bake in a preheated oven at 400°F for about 30 minutes.

6 To serve, unwrap each foil packet and serve with rice or pasta.

COOK'S TIP

To aid cooking, place the vegetables and chicken on the shiny side of the foil so that once the packet is wrapped up, the dull surface of the foil is facing outward. This ensures that the heat is absorbed into the packet and not reflected away from it.

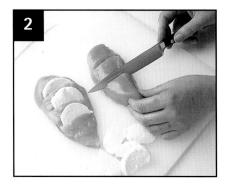

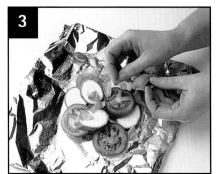

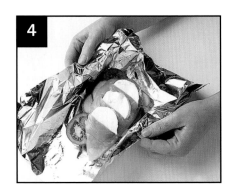

Chicken, Corn, & Snow Pea Sauté

This quick and healthy dish is stir-fried, which means you need use only the minimum of fat. If you don't have a wok, use a wide skillet instead.

Serves 4

INGREDIENTS

4 skinless, boneless
    chicken breasts
1⅓ cups baby corn
9 ounces snow peas
2 tablespoons sunflower oil
1 tablespoon sherry vinegar

1 tablespoon clear honey
1 tablespoon light soy sauce
1 tablespoon sunflower seeds
pepper
rice or egg noodles, to serve

1 Using a sharp knife, slice the chicken breasts into long, thin strips. Cut the baby corn in half lengthwise and top and tail the snow peas. Set the prepared vegetables aside until they are required.

2 Heat the sunflower oil in a wok or a wide skillet. Add the chicken and fry over fairly high heat, stirring constantly, for 1 minute.

3 Add the corn and snow peas and stir over moderate heat for 5–8 minutes, until evenly cooked through.

4 Mix together the sherry vinegar, honey, and soy sauce and stir into the pan with the sunflower seeds. Season with pepper to taste. Cook, stirring constantly, for 1 minute. Serve the sauté hot with rice or Chinese egg noodles.

COOK'S TIP

Rice vinegar or balsamic vinegar would make a good substitute for the sherry vinegar.

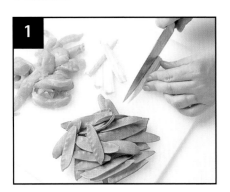

Savory Chicken Sausages

Served with a smooth creamy tomato sauce,
this makes an excellent light lunch with freshly baked cheese bread.

Serves 4–6

INGREDIENTS

3 cups fresh bread crumbs
9 ounces cooked chicken, ground
1 small leek, finely chopped
pinch of mixed herbs
pinch of mustard powder
2 eggs, separated

4 tablespoons milk
crisp bread crumbs, for coating
2 tablespoons beef drippings
salt and pepper

1 In a large mixing bowl, combine the bread crumbs, ground chicken, leek, mixed herbs, and mustard powder, and season with salt and pepper. Mix together until thoroughly incorporated.

2 Add 1 whole egg and an egg yolk with a little milk to bind the mixture.

3 Divide the mixture into 6 or 8 and shape into thick or thin sausages.

4 Whisk the remaining egg white until frothy. Coat the sausages first in the egg white, and then in the crisp bread crumbs.

5 Heat the drippings and fry the sausages for 6 minutes, until golden brown. Serve at once.

COOK'S TIP

Make your own ground chicken by working lean cuts of chicken in a food processor.

VARIATION

If you want to lower the saturated fat content of this recipe, use a little oil for frying instead of the drippings.

Golden Chicken Risotto

Risotto rice is also known as arborio rice and is available at specialty grocers. If desired, ordinary long grain rice can be used instead, but it won't give you the traditional, deliciously creamy texture.

Serves 4

INGREDIENTS

2 tablespoons sunflower oil

1 tablespoon butter
  or margarine

1 medium leek, thinly sliced

1 large yellow bell pepper, diced

3 skinless, boneless chicken
  breasts, diced

12 ounces risotto rice

few strands saffron

$6\frac{1}{4}$ cups chicken stock

7 ounce can corn

$\frac{1}{2}$ cup toasted
  unsalted peanuts

$\frac{1}{2}$ cup grated Parmesan cheese

salt and pepper

---

1 Heat the oil and butter or margarine in a large saucepan. Fry the leek and bell pepper for 1 minute, then stir in the chicken, and cook, stirring until golden brown.

2 Stir in the rice and cook for 2–3 minutes.

3 Stir in the saffron strands and salt and pepper to taste. Add the stock, a little at a time, cover, and cook over low heat, stirring occasionally, for about 20 minutes, until the rice is tender and most of the liquid has been absorbed. Do not let the risotto dry out—add more stock if necessary.

4 Stir in the corn, peanuts, and Parmesan cheese, then adjust the seasoning to taste. Serve the risotto hot.

COOK'S TIP

Risottos can be frozen, before adding the Parmesan cheese, for up to 1 month, but remember to reheat this risotto thoroughly as it contains chicken.

Quick Chicken Bake

This recipe is a type of shepherd's pie and is just as versatile. Add vegetables and herbs of your choice, depending on what you have to hand.

Serves 4

INGREDIENTS

1 pound 2 ounces ground chicken
1 large onion, finely chopped
2 carrots, finely diced
2 tablespoons all-
   purpose flour
1 tablespoon tomato paste
1^1/$_4$ cups chicken stock
pinch of fresh thyme

2 pounds potatoes, creamed with
   butter and milk and highly
   seasoned
^{3}/$_4$ cup grated semihard white cheese
salt and pepper
peas, to serve

1 Brown the ground chicken, onion, and carrots in a nonstick saucepan for 5 minutes, stirring frequently.

2 Sprinkle the chicken with the flour and simmer for a further 2 minutes.

3 Gradually blend in the tomato paste and stock, then simmer for 15 minutes. Season and add the thyme.

4 Transfer the chicken and vegetable mixture to an ovenproof casserole and set aside to cool.

5 Spoon the mashed potato over the chicken mixture and sprinkle with the cheese. Bake in a preheated oven at 400°F for 20 minutes, or until the cheese is bubbling and golden, then serve, straight from the casserole, with the peas.

VARIATION

Instead of plain cheese, you could sprinkle a flavored cheese over the top. There are a variety of cheeses blended with onion and chives, and these are ideal for melting as a topping. Alternatively, you could use a mixture of cheeses, depending on whatever you have on hand.

Tom's Toad in the Hole

*This unusual recipe uses chicken and Cumberland sausage,
which is then made into individual bite-size cakes.*

Serves 4-6

INGREDIENTS

1 cup plain all-purpose flour
pinch of salt
1 egg, beaten

1 scant cup milk
$1/3$ cup water
2 tablespoons beef drippings

9 ounces chicken breasts
9 ounces Cumberland sausage

1 Mix the flour and salt in a bowl, make a well in the center, and add the beaten egg.

2 Add half the milk, and using a wooden spoon, gradually work in the flour.

3 Beat the mixture until smooth, then add the remaining milk and water.

4 Beat again until the mixture is smooth. Set the mixture aside to stand for at least 1 hour. Add the drippings to individual baking pans or to one large baking pan.

5 Cut up the chicken and sausage so that you have a generous piece in each individual pan or several scattered around the large pan.

6 Heat the pans in a preheated oven at 425°F for 5 minutes, until very hot. Remove the pans from the oven and pour in the batter, leaving space for the mixture to expand.

7 Return to the oven to cook for 35 minutes, until risen and golden brown. While cooking, do not open the oven door for at least 30 minutes.

8 Serve hot, with chicken or onion gravy, or alone.

VARIATION

Use skinless, boneless chicken legs, instead of chicken breast, in the recipe. Cut up as directed. Instead of Cumberland sausage, use your favorite variety of sausage.

Casseroles & Roasts

Long, slow cooking means meltingly succulent meat with a good, rich flavor. Because chicken itself does not have a strong flavor, it marries happily with almost any other ingredient, herb, or spice. The recipes in this section are drawn from many cuisines from around the world, and there are dishes from Italy, France, Hungary, the Caribbean, and the United States. French classics include Bourguignonne of Chicken and Brittany Chicken Casserole.

The aroma of roasting chicken is always tempting and this section includes the traditional roast chicken, with all the trimmings, as well as many other imaginative treatments. Unusual stuffings to try are zucchini and lime, marmalade, or oat and herb stuffing. Many of the recipes in this section exploit the complementary flavors of chicken and fruits and there are some enticing taste combinations including cranberries, black cherries, apples, peaches, oranges, and mangoes.

Rustic Chicken & Orange Pot

*Low in fat and high in fiber, this colorful casserole
makes a healthy and hearty meal.*

Serves 4

INGREDIENTS

8 chicken drumsticks, skinned
1 tablespoon whole-wheat flour
1 tablespoon olive oil
2 medium red onions
1 garlic clove, crushed
1 teaspoon fennel seeds
1 bay leaf

finely grated rind and juice
  of 1 small orange
14 ounce can chopped tomatoes
14 ounce can cannellini
  or flageolet beans, drained
salt and black pepper

TOPPING:
3 thick slices whole-wheat bread
2 teaspoons olive oil

1 Toss the chicken drumsticks in the flour to coat evenly. Heat the oil in a nonstick or heavy-based saucepan and fry the chicken over fairly high heat, turning frequently, until golden brown. Transfer to a large ovenproof casserole and keep warm until required.

2 Slice the red onions into thin wedges. Add to the pan and cook for a few minutes, until lightly browned. Stir in the garlic.

3 Add the fennel seeds, bay leaf, orange rind and juice, tomatoes, beans, and seasoning.

4 Cover tightly and cook in a preheated oven at 375°F for 30–35 minutes, until the chicken juices are clear and not pink when pierced through the thickest part with the point of a sharp knife.

5 For the topping, cut the bread into small dice and toss in the oil. Remove the lid from the casserole and top with the bread cubes. Bake for a further 15–20 minutes, until the bread is golden and crisp. Serve hot.

COOK'S TIP

Choose beans which are canned in water with no added sugar or salt. Drain and rinse well before use.

Spiced Chicken Casserole

Spices, herbs, fruit, nuts, and vegetables are combined to make an appealing casserole with lots of flavor.

Serves 4–6

INGREDIENTS

3 tablespoons olive oil
2 pounds chicken meat, sliced
10 shallots or pickling onions
3 carrots, chopped
1/2 cup water chestnuts, sliced
1/2 cup slivered almonds, toasted
1 teaspoon freshly grated nutmeg
1 tablespoon ground cinnamon
1 1/4 cups white wine

1 1/4 cups chicken stock
3/4 cup white wine vinegar
1 tablespoon chopped fresh tarragon
1 tablespoon chopped fresh flat
  leaf parsley
1 tablespoon chopped fresh thyme
grated rind of 1 orange
1 tablespoon brown sugar
3/4 cup seedless black grapes, halved

sea salt and pepper
fresh herbs, to garnish
wild rice or puréed potato, to serve

1 Heat the olive oil in a large saucepan and fry the chicken, shallots or pickling onions, and carrots for about 6 minutes, or until browned.

2 Add the remaining ingredients, except the grapes, and simmer over low heat for 2 hours, until the meat is very tender. Stir the casserole occasionally.

3 Add the grapes just before serving and serve with wild rice or puréed potato. Garnish with herbs.

VARIATION

Experiment with different types of nuts and fruits—try sunflower seeds instead of the almonds, and add 2 fresh apricots, chopped.

COOK'S TIP

This casserole would also be delicious served with thick slices of crusty whole-wheat bread to soak up the sauce.

Country Chicken Hot-Pot

There are many regional versions of hot-pot, all using fresh, local ingredients. Now, there is an endless variety of ingredients available all year, perfect for traditional one-pot cooking.

Serves 4

INGREDIENTS

4 chicken quarters
6 medium potatoes, cut
   into ¼-inch slices
2 sprigs thyme
2 sprigs rosemary
2 bay leaves

1 cup diced smoked bacon
1 large onion, finely chopped
1 cup sliced carrots
⅔ cup stout or dark beer
2 tablespoons melted butter
salt and pepper

1 Remove the skin from the chicken quarters, if desired.

2 Arrange a layer of potato slices in the base of a wide casserole. Season with salt and pepper, then add the thyme, rosemary, and bay leaves.

3 Top with the chicken quarters, then sprinkle with the diced bacon, onion, and carrots. Season well and arrange the remaining potato slices on top, overlapping slightly.

4 Pour over the stout or beer, brush the potatoes with the melted butter, and cover with a lid.

5 Bake in a preheated oven at 300°F for about 2 hours, uncovering for the last 30 minutes to allow the potatoes to brown. Serve hot.

COOK'S TIP

Serve the hot-pot with dumplings for a truly hearty meal.

VARIATION

This dish is also delicious with stewing lamb, cut into chunks. You can add different vegetables, depending on what is in season try leeks and rutabaga for a slightly sweeter flavor.

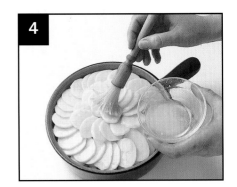

Fricassée of Chicken in Lime Sauce

The addition of lime juice and lime rind adds a delicious tangy flavor to this chicken stew.

Serves 4

INGREDIENTS

1 large chicken, cut into
  small portions
$1/2$ cup all-purpose flour, seasoned
2 tablespoons oil
1 pound 2 ounces baby onions
  or shallots, sliced

1 green bell pepper, thinly sliced
1 red bell pepper, thinly sliced
$2/3$ cup chicken stock
juice and rind of 2 limes
2 chiles, chopped
2 tablespoons oyster sauce

1 teaspoon Worcestershire sauce
salt and pepper

1 Coat the chicken pieces in the seasoned flour. Heat the oil in a large skillet and cook the chicken for about 4 minutes, until browned all over.

2 Using a slotted spoon, transfer the chicken to a large, deep casserole and sprinkle with the sliced onions. Keep warm until required.

3 Fry the bell peppers in the juices remaining in the skillet over low heat.

4 Add the chicken stock, lime juice, and rind and cook for a further 5 minutes.

5 Add the chiles, oyster sauce, and Worcestershire sauce. Season with salt and pepper to taste.

6 Pour the bell peppers and juices over the chicken and onions.

7 Cover the casserole with a lid or cooking foil.

8 Cook in the center of a preheated oven at 375°F for $1\frac{1}{2}$ hours, until the chicken is very tender, then serve.

COOK'S TIP

Try this casserole with a cheese biscuit topping. About 30 minutes before the end of cooking time, simply top with a layer of rounds cut from ready-made biscuit pastry, and shredded cheese.

Bourguignonne of Chicken

A recipe based on a classic French dish. Use a good-quality wine when making this casserole.

Serves 4-6

INGREDIENTS

4 tablespoons sunflower oil
2 pounds chicken meat, diced
3 cups button mushrooms
$^2/_3$ cup diced smoked bacon
16 baby onions
2 garlic cloves, crushed
1 tablespoon all-purpose flour

$^2/_3$ cup white Burgundy wine
$^2/_3$ cup chicken stock
1 bouquet garni (1 bay leaf, sprig thyme, stalk of celery, parsley, and sage tied with string)
salt and pepper

deep-fried croûtons and a selection of cooked vegetables, to serve

1 Heat the sunflower oil in a flameproof casserole and brown the chicken all over. Remove from the casserole with a slotted spoon.

2 Add the mushrooms, bacon, onions, and garlic to the casserole and cook for 4 minutes.

3 Return the chicken to the casserole and sprinkle with flour. Cook for a further 2 minutes, stirring.

4 Add the Burgundy wine and chicken stock to the casserole and stir until the mixture comes to a boil. Add the bouquet garni and season to taste with salt and pepper.

5 Cover the casserole and bake in the center of a preheated oven at 300°F for 1½ hours. Remove the bouquet garni.

6 Deep fry some heart-shaped croûtons (about 8 large ones)

in beef drippings and serve with the bourguignonne.

COOK'S TIP

A good-quality red wine can be used instead of the white wine, to produce a rich, glossy red sauce.

Country Chicken Bake

This economical bake is a complete meal—its crusty, herb-flavored French bread topping mops up the tasty juices, and means there's no need to serve potatoes or rice separately.

Serves 4

INGREDIENTS

2 tablespoons sunflower oil

4 chicken quarters

16 small whole onions, peeled

3 stalks celery, sliced

14 ounce can red kidney beans

4 medium tomatoes, quartered

scant 1 cup hard cider or stock

4 tablespoons chopped fresh parsley

1 teaspoon paprika

4 tablespoons butter

12 slices French bread

salt and pepper

1 Heat the oil in a flameproof casserole and fry the chicken quarters, two at a time, until golden. Using a slotted spoon, remove the chicken from the pan and set aside until required.

2 Add the onions and fry, turning occasionally, until golden brown. Add the celery and fry for 2–3 minutes. Return the chicken to the pan, then stir in the beans, tomatoes, cider, and half the parsley, and season to taste. Sprinkle with the paprika.

3 Cover and cook in a preheated oven at 400°F for 20–25 minutes, until the juices run clear when the chicken is pierced with the point of a sharp knife.

4 Mix the remaining parsley with the butter and spread it evenly over the French bread.

5 Uncover the casserole, arrange the bread slices overlapping on top, and bake for a further 10–12 minutes, until golden and crisp.

COOK'S TIP

Add a crushed garlic clove to the parsley butter for extra flavor.

VARIATION

For a more Italian-tasting dish, replace the garlic and parsley bread topping with Pesto Toasts (see page 208).

Hungarian Chicken Goulash

*Goulash is traditionally made with beef, but this recipe successfully uses chicken instead.
To reduce fat, use a reduced-fat cream in place of the sour cream.*

Serves 6

INGREDIENTS

2 pounds chicken meat, diced
$\frac{1}{2}$ cup all-purpose flour, seasoned
   with 1 teaspoon paprika, salt
   and pepper
2 tablespoons olive oil
2 tablespoons butter
1 onion, sliced

24 baby onions, peeled
1 each red and green
   bell peppers, chopped
1 tablespoon paprika
1 teaspoon rosemary, crushed
4 tablespoons tomato paste
$1\frac{1}{4}$ cups chicken stock

$\frac{2}{3}$ cup claret, or other dry red wine
14 ounce can chopped tomatoes
$\frac{2}{3}$ cup sour cream
1 tablespoon chopped fresh parsley,
   to garnish
chunks of bread and a side salad,
   to serve

1 Toss the chicken in the seasoned flour until it is coated all over.

2 In a flameproof casserole, heat the oil and butter and fry the onion, baby onions and bell peppers for 3 minutes.

3 Add the chicken and cook for a further 4 minutes.

4 Sprinkle with the paprika and rosemary.

5 Add the tomato paste, chicken stock, claret, and chopped tomatoes, cover, and cook in the center of a preheated oven at 325°F for 1½ hours.

6 Remove the casserole from the oven, set aside to stand for about 4 minutes, then add the sour cream and garnish with parsley.

7 Serve straight from the casserole with chunks of bread and a side salad.

VARIATION

Serve the goulash with buttered ribbon noodles instead of bread. For an authentic touch, try a Hungarian red wine, instead of the claret.

Country Chicken Braise with Rosemary Dumplings

Root vegetables are always cheap and nutritious, and combined with chicken they make tasty and economical casseroles.

Serves 4

INGREDIENTS

4 chicken quarters
2 tablespoons sunflower oil
2 medium leeks
1 cup chopped carrots
2 cups chopped parsnips
2 small turnips, chopped

2^1/$_2$ cups chicken stock
3 tablespoons Worcestershire sauce
2 sprigs fresh rosemary
salt and pepper

DUMPLINGS:
1^3/$_4$ cups self-rising flour
3^1/$_2$ oz lard
1 tablespoon chopped rosemary
  leaves
cold water, to mix

1 Remove the skin from the chicken, if desired. Heat the oil in a large, flameproof casserole or heavy-based saucepan and fry the chicken until golden brown all over. Using a slotted spoon, remove the chicken from the pan. Drain off the excess fat.

2 Trim and slice the leeks. Add the carrots, parsnips, and turnips to the casserole and cook for 5 minutes, until lightly

colored. Return the chicken to the pan.

3 Add the chicken stock, Worcestershire sauce, rosemary, and seasoning, then bring to a boil.

4 Reduce the heat, cover, and simmer gently for about 50 minutes, or until the juices run clear when the chicken is pierced with the point of a sharp knife.

5 To make the dumplings, combine the flour, suet, and rosemary leaves with salt and pepper in a bowl. Stir in just enough cold water to bind to a firm dough.

6 Form into 8 small balls and place on top of the chicken and vegetables. Cover and simmer for a further 10–12 minutes, until the dumplings are well risen. Serve with the casserole.

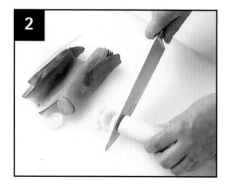

Chicken in Exotic Mushroom & Ginger Sauce

This recipe has a southeast Asian flavor, which can be further enhanced with chopped scallions, cinnamon, and lemon grass.

Serves 6–8

INGREDIENTS

6 tablespoons sesame oil
2 pounds chicken meat
$^1/_2$ cup all-purpose flour, seasoned
32 baby onions, sliced
6 cups roughly chopped exotic
  mushrooms

$1^1/_4$ cups chicken stock
2 tablespoons Worcestershire sauce
1 tablespoon clear honey
2 tablespoons grated fresh
  ginger root
$^2/_3$ cup unsweetened yogurt

salt and pepper
flat leaf parsley, to garnish
wild rice and white rice, to serve

1 Heat the oil in a large skillet. Coat the chicken in the seasoned flour and cook for about 4 minutes, until browned all over. Transfer to a large deep casserole and keep warm until required.

2 Add the baby onions and mushrooms to the juices in the skillet and fry over a low heat.

3 Add the chicken stock, Worcestershire sauce, honey, and fresh ginger, then season to taste with salt and pepper.

4 Pour the mixture over the chicken, and cover the casserole with a lid or cooking foil.

5 Cook in the center of a preheated oven at 300°F for about 1½ hours, until the meat is very tender. Add the yogurt and cook for a further 10 minutes. Serve the casserole with a mixture of wild rice and white rice, and garnish with fresh parsley.

COOK'S TIP

Mushrooms can be stored in the refrigerator for 24–36 hours. Keep them in paper bags as they "sweat" in plastic. You do not need to peel mushrooms, but wild mushrooms must be washed thoroughly.

Jamaican Hot-Pot

A tasty way to make chicken cuts go a long way, this hearty casserole, spiced with the warm, subtle flavor of ginger, is a good choice for a Halloween party.

Serves 4

INGREDIENTS

2 teaspoons sunflower oil
4 chicken drumsticks
4 chicken thighs
1 medium onion
1 pound 10 ounces piece squash
   or pumpkin
1 green bell pepper

1-inch fresh ginger root,
   finely chopped
14 ounce can chopped
   tomatoes
1¼ cups chicken stock
¼ cup lentils
garlic salt

cayenne pepper
12 ounce can corn
crusty bread, to serve

1 Heat the oil in a large flameproof casserole and fry the chicken joints until golden, turning frequently.

2 Using a sharp knife, peel and slice the onion, peel and dice the pumpkin or squash, and seed and slice the bell pepper.

3 Drain any excess fat from the pan and add the prepared onion, pumpkin, and bell pepper. Gently fry for a few minutes until lightly browned. Add the chopped ginger, tomatoes, chicken stock, and lentils. Season lightly with garlic salt and cayenne pepper.

4 Cover the casserole and cook in a preheated oven at 375°F for about 1 hour, until the vegetables are tender and the juices run clear when the chicken is pierced with the point of a knife.

5 Add the drained corn and cook for a further 5 minutes. Season to taste and serve with crusty bread.

VARIATION

If you can't find fresh ginger root, add 1 teaspoon allspice for a warm, fragrant aroma.

VARIATION

If squash or pumpkin is not available, rutabaga makes a good substitute.

Garlic Chicken Casserole

This is a cassoulet with a twist—it is made with chicken instead of duck and lamb. Save time by using canned beans, such as borlotti or cannellini beans, which are both good in this dish.

Serves 4

INGREDIENTS

4 tablespoons sunflower oil
2 pounds chicken meat, chopped
3 cups sliced mushrooms
16 shallots
6 garlic cloves, crushed
1 tablespoon all-purpose flour

1 cup white wine
1 cup chicken stock
1 bouquet garni (1 bay leaf, sprig
    thyme, celery, parsley and sage tied
    with string)
14 ounce can cannellini beans

salt and pepper
pattypan squash, to serve

---

1 Heat the sunflower oil in a flameproof casserole and fry the chicken until browned all over. Remove the chicken from the casserole with a slotted spoon and set aside until required.

2 Add the mushrooms, shallots, and garlic to the oil in the casserole and cook for 4 minutes.

3 Return the chicken to the casserole, sprinkle with the flour, then cook for a further 2 minutes.

4 Add the white wine and chicken stock, stir until boiling, then add the bouquet garni. Season well with salt and pepper.

5 Drain the beans and rinse thoroughly, then add to the casserole.

6 Cover and place in the center of a preheated oven at 300°F for 2 hours. Remove and discard the bouquet garni and serve the casserole with pattypan squash.

COOK'S TIP

Mushrooms are ideal in a low-fat diet because they are high in flavor and contain no fat. Experiment with the wealth of varieties that are now available from supermarkets.

COOK'S TIP

Serve the casserole with brown rice to make this filling dish go even further.

Old English Chicken Stewed in Ale

A slow-cooked, old-fashioned stew to warm up a wintery day. The rarebit toasts are a perfect accompaniment to soak up the rich juices, but if desired, serve the stew with baked potatoes.

Serves 4-6

INGREDIENTS

4 large, skinless chicken thighs
2 tablespoons all-purpose flour
2 tablespoons English
   mustard powder
2 tablespoons sunflower oil
1 tablespoon butter
4 small onions

2^1/2 cups beer
2 tablespoons Worcestershire sauce
3 tablespoons chopped fresh
   sage leaves
salt and pepper

RAREBIT TOASTS:
^{1}/2 cup grated sharp cheddar cheese
1 teaspoon English mustard powder
1 teaspoon all-purpose flour
1 teaspoon Worcestershire sauce
1 tablespoon beer
2 slices whole wheat toast

1   Trim any excess fat from the chicken and toss in the flour and mustard powder to coat evenly. Heat the sunflower oil and butter in a large flameproof casserole and fry the chicken over a fairly high heat, turning occasionally, until golden. Remove from the casserole with a slotted spoon and keep hot.

2   Peel and slice the onions into wedges and fry quickly until golden. Add the chicken, beer, Worcestershire sauce, fresh sage, salt, and pepper. Bring to a boil, cover, and simmer very gently for about 1½ hours, until the chicken is very tender.

3   Meanwhile, make the rarebit toasts: mix the cheese with the mustard powder, flour, Worcestershire sauce, and beer. Spread over the toasts and place under a hot broiler for about 1 minute, until melted and golden. Cut into triangles.

4   Stir the sage leaves into the chicken stew, bring to a boil, and serve with the rarebit toasts, a green vegetable, and new potatoes.

COOK'S TIP

If you do not have fresh sage, use 2 teaspoons of dried sage in step 2.

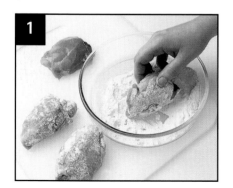

Brittany Chicken Casserole

A hearty, one-dish meal that would make a substantial lunch or supper. As it requires a long cooking time, make double quantities and freeze half to eat later.

Serves 6

INGREDIENTS

2^1/$_2$ cups beans, such as small navy beans, soaked overnight and drained
2 tablespoons butter
2 tablespoons olive oil
3 bacon slices, chopped

2 pounds chicken pieces
1 tablespoon all-purpose flour
1^1/$_4$ cups cider
^{2}/$_3$ cup chicken stock
14 baby onions
2 tablespoons honey, warmed

8 oz cooked beet
salt and pepper

1 Cook the beans in salted boiling water for about 25 minutes.

2 Heat the butter and olive oil in a flameproof casserole, add the bacon and chicken, and cook for 5 minutes.

3 Sprinkle with the flour, then add the cider and chicken stock, stirring constantly to avoid lumps forming. Season with salt and pepper to taste and bring the mixture to a boil.

4 Add the beans, then cover the casserole tightly with a lid or cooking foil, and bake in the center of a preheated oven at 325°F for 2 hours.

5 About 15 minutes before the end of cooking time, remove the lid or cooking foil from the casserole.

6 In a skillet, cook the baby onions and honey together over low heat for 5 minutes, turning the onions frequently.

7 Add the baby onions and cooked beet to the casserole and leave to finish cooking in the oven for the last 15 minutes.

COOK'S TIP

To save time, use canned beans instead of dried. Drain and rinse before adding to the chicken.

Rich Mediterranean Chicken Casserole

A colorful casserole packed with sunshine flavors from the Mediterranean.
Sun-dried tomatoes add a wonderful richness and you need very few to make this dish really special.

Serves 4

INGREDIENTS

8 chicken thighs
2 tablespoons olive oil
1 medium red onion, sliced
2 garlic cloves, crushed
1 large red bell pepper, sliced thickly
thinly pared rind and juice
  of 1 small orange
$^1/_2$ cup chicken stock

14 ounce can chopped tomatoes
$^1/_2$ cup thinly sliced sun-
  dried tomatoes
1 tablespoon chopped fresh thyme
$^1/_2$ cup pitted black olives
salt and pepper

thyme sprigs and orange
  rind, to garnish
crusty fresh bread, to serve

1 In a heavy or nonstick large skillet, fry the chicken without fat over fairly high heat, turning occasionally, until golden brown. Using a slotted spoon, drain off any excess fat from the chicken and transfer it to a flameproof casserole.

2 Fry the onion, garlic, and bell pepper in the skillet over moderate heat for 3–4 minutes. Transfer to the casserole.

3 Add the orange rind and juice, chicken stock, canned tomatoes, and sun-dried tomatoes and stir to combine.

4 Bring to a boil, then cover the casserole with a lid, and simmer very gently over low heat for about 1 hour, stirring occasionally. Add the chopped fresh thyme and pitted black olives, then adjust the seasoning if necessary.

5 Scatter the orange rind and thyme over the casserole to garnish, and serve with fresh bread.

COOK'S TIP

Sun-dried tomatoes have a dense texture and concentrated taste, and add intense flavor to slow-cooking casseroles.

Chicken Madeira "French-style"

*Madeira is a fortified wine which can be used in both sweet and savory dishes.
Here, it adds a rich, full flavor to the casserole.*

Serves 8

INGREDIENTS

2 tablespoons butter
20 baby onions
1¹/₂ cups sliced carrots
1¹/₂ cups chopped bacon
3 cups button mushrooms

1 chicken, weighing about
  3 pounds 5 ounces
scant 2 cups white wine
¹/₄ cup seasoned all-purpose flour
scant 2 cups chicken stock
bouquet garni

²/₃ cup Madeira wine
salt and pepper
mashed potato or pasta, to serve

1 Heat the butter in a large skillet and fry the onions, carrots, bacon, and button mushrooms for 3 minutes, stirring frequently. Transfer to a large casserole dish.

2 Add the chicken to the skillet and brown all over. Transfer to the casserole dish with the vegetables and bacon.

3 Add the white wine and cook until the wine is nearly completely reduced.

4 Sprinkle with the seasoned flour, stirring to prevent lumps from forming.

5 Add the chicken stock, salt, and pepper to taste, and the bouquet garni. Cover and cook the casserole for 2 hours. About 30 minutes before the end of cooking time, add the Madeira wine and continue cooking uncovered.

6 Carve the chicken and serve with mashed potato or pasta.

COOK'S TIP

You can add any combination of herbs to this recipe—chervil is a popular herb in French cuisine, but add it at the end of cooking, so that its delicate flavor is not lost. Other herbs which work well with chicken are parsley and tarragon.

Springtime Chicken Cobbler

Fresh spring vegetables are the basis of this colorful casserole, which is topped with hearty whole-wheat dumplings for a complete, healthy family meal.

Serves 4

INGREDIENTS

8 skinless chicken drumsticks
1 tablespoon oil
1 small onion, sliced
1½ cups baby carrots
2 baby turnips
1 cup fava beans or peas
1 teaspoon cornstarch
1¼ cups chicken stock

2 bay leaves
salt and pepper

COBBLER TOPPING:
2 cups whole-wheat all-purpose flour
2 teaspoon baking powder

2 tablespoons sunflower soft margarine
2 teaspoons dry wholegrain mustard
½ cup grated Cheddar cheese
skim milk, to mix
sesame seeds, to sprinkle

1 Fry the chicken in the oil, turning, until golden brown. Drain well and place in a casserole. Sauté the onion for 2–3 minutes to soften.

2 Wash and trim the carrots and turnips and cut into equal-size pieces. Add to the casserole with the onions and beans or peas.

3 Blend the cornstarch with a little of the stock, then stir in the rest and heat gently, stirring until boiling. Pour into the casserole and add the bay leaves, salt, and pepper.

4 Cover tightly and bake in a preheated oven at 400°F for 50–60 minutes, or until the juices run clear when the chicken is pierced with the point of a knife.

5 For the topping, sift the flour and baking powder. Mix in the margarine with a fork. Stir in the mustard, the cheese and enough milk to form a fairly soft dough.

6 Roll out and cut 16 rounds with a 1½-inch cutter. Uncover the casserole, arrange the biscuit rounds on top, then brush with milk, and sprinkle with sesame seeds. Bake in the oven for 20 minutes, or until the topping is golden and firm.

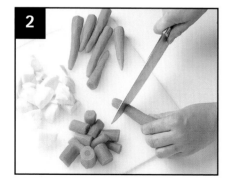

California Chicken

It is better if you have time to bone the chicken completely,
or use chicken breast after removing all the fat and skin.

Serves 4-6

INGREDIENTS

1¹/₂ cups plain all-purpose flour
1 teaspoon paprika
1 teaspoon dried Italian seasoning
1 teaspoon dried tarragon
1 teaspoon rosemary, finely crushed
2 eggs, beaten
¹/₂ cup milk

1 chicken, weighing about
  4 pounds, cut into pieces
seasoned flour
²/₃ cup canola oil
2 bananas, quartered
1 apple, cut into rings,

12 ounce can mixed corn and bell
  peppers, drained
oil for frying
salt and pepper
watercress, and peppercorn or
  horseradish sauce, to serve

1 Mix together the flour, spices, herbs, and a pinch of salt in a large bowl. Make a well in the center and add the eggs.

2 Blend and gradually add the milk, whisking until the batter is very smooth.

3 Coat the chicken pieces with seasoned flour and dip the chicken pieces into the batter mix.

4 Heat the oil in a large skillet. Add the chicken and fry for

about 3 minutes, or until lightly browned all over. Place the chicken pieces on a nonstick cookie sheet.

5 Batter the bananas and apple rings and fry for 2 minutes.

6 Finally toss the mixed corn and bell peppers into the leftover batter.

7 Heat a little oil in a skillet. Drop in spoonfuls of the corn mixture to make fritters. Cook for

4 minutes on each side. Remove from the skillet and keep warm with the apple and banana fritters.

8 Bake the chicken in a preheated oven at 400°F for about 25 minutes, until it is cooked through, tender and golden brown.

9 Arrange the chicken, corn fritters, and apple and banana fritters on a bed of fresh watercress. Serve with a peppercorn or horseradish sauce.

Chicken with Baby Onions & Green Peas

Pork fat adds a tasty flavor to this dish. If you can't find fresh garden peas, frozen peas are a good substitute.

Serves 4

INGREDIENTS

1 cup diced pork fat	2¹/₄ pounds boneless	bouquet garni
4 tablespoons butter	chicken pieces	4 cups fresh peas
16 small onions	¹/₄ cup all-purpose flour	salt and pepper
or shallots	2¹/₂ cups chicken stock	

1 Bring a saucepan of salted water to a boil and simmer the pork fat cubes for three minutes. Drain and dry the pork on absorbent paper towels.

2 Melt the butter in a large skillet, add the pork and onions, and fry gently for 3 minutes, until lightly browned.

3 Remove the pork and onions from the skillet and set aside until required. Add the chicken pieces to the skillet and cook until browned all over. Transfer the chicken to a casserole.

4 Add the flour to the skillet and cook, stirring until it begins to brown, then slowly blend in the chicken stock.

5 Cook the chicken, with the sauce and bouquet garni, in a preheated oven at 400°F for 35 minutes.

6 Remove the bouquet garni about 10 minutes before the end of cooking time and add the peas and the reserved pork and onions. Stir to mix.

7 When cooked, place the chicken pieces on a large platter, surrounded by the pork, peas, and onions.

COOK'S TIP

If you want to cut down on fat, use lean bacon, cut into small cubes, rather than pork fat.

Festive Apple Chicken

The richly-flavored stuffing in this recipe is cooked under the breast skin of the chicken,
so not only is all the flavor sealed in, but the chicken stays really moist and succulent during cooking.

Serves 6

INGREDIENTS

1 chicken, weighing 4^1/2 pounds
2 apples
1 tablespoon butter
1 tablespoon red currant jelly
mixed vegetables, to serve

STUFFING:
1 tablespoon butter
1 small onion, finely chopped
^{3}/4 cup finely chopped mushrooms
^{1}/3 cup finely chopped smoked ham
^{1}/2 cup fresh bread crumbs
1 tablespoon chopped fresh parsley

1 crisp apple
1 tablespoon lemon juice
oil, for brushing
salt and pepper
mixed vegetables, to serve

1 To make the stuffing, melt the butter and fry the onion gently, stirring until softened, but not browned. Stir in the mushrooms and cook for 2–3 minutes. Remove from the heat and stir in the ham, bread crumbs and chopped parsley.

2 Core the apple, leaving the skin on, and grate coarsely. Add the stuffing mixture to the apple, together with the lemon juice. Season to taste.

3 Loosen the breast skin of the chicken and carefully spoon the stuffing mixture under it, smoothing the skin over evenly with your hands.

4 Place the chicken in a roasting pan and brush lightly all over with oil.

5 Roast the chicken in a preheated oven at 375°F for 2–2½ hours, or until there is no trace of pink in the juices when the chicken is pierced through the thickest part with the point of a sharp knife. If the breast starts to brown too much, cover the chicken with foil.

6 Core and slice the remaining apples and sauté in the butter until golden. Stir in the red currant jelly and warm through until melted. Garnish the chicken with the apple slices and serve at once with mixed vegetables.

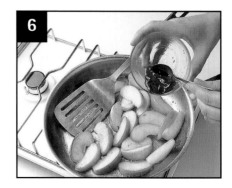

Roast Chicken with Cilantro & Garlic

This recipe for chicken is coated with a fresh-flavored marinade then roasted. Try serving it with rice, yogurt, and salad.

Serves 4-6

INGREDIENTS

3 sprigs fresh cilantro, chopped	4 tablespoons lemon juice	sprig of fresh parsley, to garnish
4 garlic cloves	4 tablespoons olive oil	boiled potatoes and carrots, to serve
1/2 teaspoon salt	1 large chicken	
1 teaspoon pepper	pepper	

1 Place the chopped cilantro, garlic, salt, pepper, lemon juice, and olive oil in a pestle and pound together with a mortar or process in a food processor. Chill in the refrigerator for 4 hours to allow the flavors to develop.

2 Place the chicken in a roasting pan. Coat generously with the cilantro and garlic mixture.

3 Sprinkle with pepper and roast in a preheated oven at 375°F on a low shelf for 1½ hours, basting every 20 minutes with the cilantro mixture. If the chicken starts to turn brown, cover with foil. Transfer to a carving dish, garnish with fresh parsley and serve with the potatoes and carrots.

COOK'S TIP

For pounding small quantities, it is best to use a pestle and mortar so as little as possible of the mixture is left in the container.

VARIATION

Any fresh herb can be used in this recipe instead of the cilantro. Tarragon or thyme make a good combination with chicken.

Feta Chicken with Mountain Herbs

Chicken goes well with most savory herbs, especially during the summer, when fresh herbs are at their best. This combination makes a good partner for tangy feta cheese and sun-ripened tomatoes.

Serves 4

INGREDIENTS

8 skinless, boneless chicken thighs
2 tablespoons each chopped fresh
   thyme, rosemary, and oregano
4¹/₂ oz feta cheese
1 tablespoon milk
2 tablespoons all-purpose flour
salt and pepper

thyme, rosemary, and oregano,
   to garnish

TOMATO SAUCE:
1 medium onion, roughly chopped
1 garlic clove, crushed
1 tablespoon olive oil
4 medium plum tomatoes, quartered

sprig each of thyme, rosemary,
   and oregano

1 Spread out the chicken thighs on a board, smooth side downward.

2 Divide the herbs among the chicken thighs, then cut the cheese into eight sticks. Place one stick of cheese in the center of each chicken thigh. Season well, then roll up to enclose the cheese.

3 Place the rolls in an ovenproof dish, brush with milk, and dust with flour to coat evenly.

4 Bake in a preheated oven at 375°F for 25–30 minutes, or until golden brown. The juices should run clear and not pink when the chicken is pierced with the point of a sharp knife in the thickest part.

5 To make the sauce, cook the onion and garlic in the olive oil, stirring, until softened and just beginning to brown.

6 Add the tomatoes, reduce the heat, cover, and simmer for 15–20 minutes, or until soft.

7 Add the herbs, transfer to a food processor, and process to a purée. Press through a strainer to make a smooth, rich sauce. Season to taste and serve the sauce with the chicken, garnished with herbs.

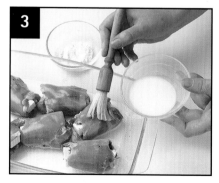

Rock Cornish Hens with Dried Fruits

Rock Cornish hens are ideal for a one- or two-portion meal, and cook very easily and quickly for a special dinner. If you're cooking for one, a microwave makes cooking even quicker.

Serves 2

INGREDIENTS

$^3/_4$ cup dried apples,
   peaches, and prunes
$^1/_2$ cup boiling water
2 rock Cornish hens
$^1/_3$ cup walnut halves

1 tablespoon clear honey
1 teaspoon ground allspice
1 tablespoon walnut oil

salt and pepper
fresh vegetables and new potatoes,
   to serve

1 Place the dried fruits in a bowl, cover with the boiling water, and let stand for about 30 minutes.

2 Cut the rock Cornish hens in half down the breastbone using a sharp knife, or leave them whole, if desired.

3 Mix the fruit and any juices remaining in the bowl with the walnut halves, honey, and ground allspice and divide the mixture among two small roasting bags or squares of foil.

4 Brush the chickens with walnut oil and sprinkle with salt and pepper, then place on top of the fruits.

5 Close the roasting bags or fold the foil over to enclose the rock Cornish hens and bake on a cookie sheet in a preheated oven at 375°F for 25–30 minutes, or until the juices run clear and not pink when the hens are pierced in the thickest part with the point of a sharp knife. To cook in a microwave, use microwave roasting bags and cook on high or 100% power for 6–7 minutes each, depending on size.

6 Serve hot with fresh vegetables and new potatoes.

COOK'S TIP

Alternative dried fruits that can be used in this recipe are cherries, mangoes or pawpaws.

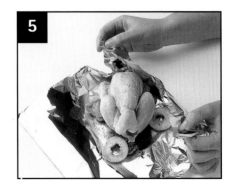

Chicken with Marmalade Stuffing

Marmalade lovers will enjoy this festive recipe. You can use any favorite marmalade, such as lemon or grapefruit.

Serves 6

INGREDIENTS

1 chicken, weighing about 5 pounds
bay leaves

STUFFING:
1 stalk celery, finely chopped
1 small onion, finely chopped
1 tablespoon sunflower oil

2 cups fresh whole wheat
bread crumbs
4 tablespoons marmalade
2 tablespoons chopped fresh parsley
1 egg, beaten
salt and pepper

SAUCE:
2 teaspoon cornstarch
2 tablespoons orange juice
3 tablespoons marmalade
$^2/_3$ cup chicken stock
1 medium orange
2 tablespoons brandy

1 Lift the neck flap of the chicken and remove the wishbone using a small, sharp knife. Place a sprig of bay leaves inside the body cavity.

2 For the stuffing, sauté the celery and onion in the oil to soften. Add the bread crumbs, 3 tablespoons of marmalade, the parsley, and egg. Season and use to stuff the neck cavity of the chicken. Any extra stuffing may be cooked separately.

3 Place the chicken in a roasting pan and brush lightly with oil. Roast in a preheated oven at 375°F for 1½–2 hours, or until the juices run clear when the chicken is pierced in the thickest part with the point of a sharp knife. Remove from the oven and glaze with the remaining marmalade.

4 Meanwhile, to make the sauce, blend the cornstarch in a pan with the orange juice, then add the marmalade and chicken

stock. Heat gently, stirring, until thickened and smooth. Remove from the heat. Cut the segments from the orange, discarding all the white pith and membrane. Just before serving, add the orange segments and brandy to the sauce and bring to a boil.

5 Serve the chicken with the orange sauce, any extra stuffing, and new potatoes.

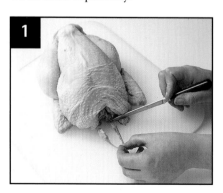

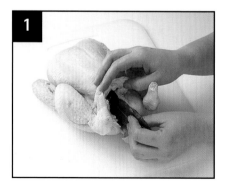

Golden Chicken with Mango & Cranberries

This recipe, which uses a partly-boned chicken, is easy to slice and serve. If you prefer, stuff in the traditional way at the neck end, and cook any remaining stuffing separately.

Serves 6

INGREDIENTS

1 chicken, weighing about 5 pounds
6 slices smoked bacon

STUFFING:
1 ripe mango, diced
1/4 cup fresh or frozen cranberries
2 cups bread crumbs

1/2 teaspoon ground mace
1 egg, beaten
salt and pepper
seasonal vegetables, to serve

GLAZE:
1/2 teaspoon ground turmeric
2 teaspoons clear honey
2 teaspoons sunflower oil

1 To partially bone the chicken, dislocate the legs and place the chicken breast side downward. Cut a straight line through the skin along the ridge of the back. Scrape the meat down from the bone on both sides.

2 When you reach the point where the legs and wings join the body, cut through the joints. Work around the ribcage until the carcass can be lifted away.

3 Make six bacon rolls. For the stuffing, mix the mango with the cranberries, bread crumbs, and mace, then bind with egg. Season.

4 Place the chicken, skin side down, and spoon over half the stuffing. Arrange the bacon rolls down the center, then top with the remaining stuffing. Fold the skin over and tie with string. Turn the chicken over, truss the legs, and tuck the wings underneath. Place

in a roasting pan. To make the glaze, mix the turmeric, honey, and oil and brush over the skin.

5 Roast in a preheated oven at 375°F for 1½–2 hours or until the juices run clear, not pink, when the chicken is pierced with the point of a sharp knife. When the chicken starts to brown, cover loosely with foil to prevent overbrowning. Serve the chicken hot with seasonal vegetables.

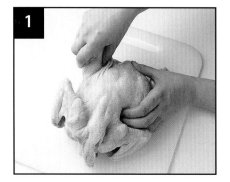

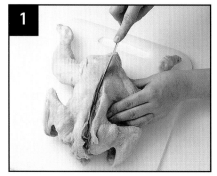

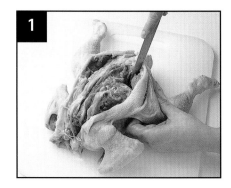

Roast Chicken Breasts with Bacon Triangles

In this recipe, a tart, fruity sauce perfectly complements the chicken and drippings triangles.

Serves 8

INGREDIENTS

4 tablespoons butter
juice of 1 lemon
1 cup red currants or cranberries
1–2 tablespoons brown sugar

8 chicken breasts
16 slices of bacon
thyme
4 tablespoons beef drippings

4 slices of bread, cut into triangles
salt and pepper

1 Heat the butter in a saucepan, add the lemon juice, red currants or cranberries, brown sugar, and salt and pepper. Cook for 1 minute and set aside to cool until required.

2 Meanwhile, season the chicken with salt and pepper. Wrap 2 slices of bacon around each breast and sprinkle with a little thyme.

3 Wrap each breast in a piece of lightly greased foil and place

in a roasting pan. Roast in a preheated oven at 400°F for 15 minutes. Remove the foil and roast the chicken for another 10 minutes.

4 Heat the drippings in a skillet and fry the bread triangles on both sides until golden brown.

5 Arrange the triangles on a large warm serving plate and top each with a chicken breast. Serve at once with a spoonful of the fruit sauce.

COOK'S TIP

You can use either chopped fresh thyme or dried thyme in this recipe, but remember that dried herbs have a stronger flavor so you need only half the quantity compared to fresh herbs.

Pollo Catalan

The Catalan region of Spain is famous for its wonderful combinations of meat with fruit. In this recipe, peaches lend a touch of sweetness, and pine nuts, cinnamon, and sherry add an unusual twist.

Serves 6

INGREDIENTS

1 cup fresh brown
   bread crumbs
½ cup pine nuts
1 small egg, beaten
4 tablespoons chopped fresh thyme
   or 1 tablespoon dried thyme

4 fresh peaches or
   8 canned peach halves
1 chicken, weighing about
   5½ pounds
1 teaspoon ground cinnamon
¾ cup Amontillado sherry

4 tablespoons heavy cream
salt and pepper

1 Combine the bread crumbs with ¼ cup of the pine nuts, the egg, and thyme.

2 Halve and pit the peaches, removing the skin if necessary. Dice one peach into small pieces and stir into the bread crumb mixture. Season well. Spoon the stuffing into the neck cavity of the chicken, securing the skin firmly over it.

3 Place the chicken in a roasting pan. Sprinkle the cinnamon over the skin.

4 Cover the chicken loosely with foil and roast in a preheated oven at 375°F for 1 hour, basting occasionally.

5 Remove the foil and spoon the sherry over the chicken. Cook for a further 30 minutes, basting with the sherry, until the juices run clear when the chicken is pierced in the thickest part with the point of a sharp knife.

6 Sprinkle the remaining pine nuts over the remaining peach halves and place in an ovenproof dish in the oven for the final 10 minutes of cooking time.

7 Lift the chicken onto a serving plate and arrange the peach halves around it. Skim any fat from the juices, stir in the cream and heat gently. Serve with the chicken.

COOK'S TIP

Canned apricot halves in natural juice are an easy cupboard alternative.

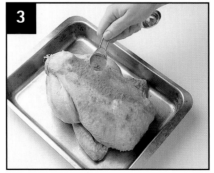

Breasts of Chicken with Black Cherries

*This recipe is rather time-consuming but it is well worth the effort.
Cherries and chicken make a good flavor combination.*

Serves 6

INGREDIENTS

6 large chicken breasts
6 black peppercorns, crushed
2 cups pitted black cherries, or
   canned pitted cherries
1–2 shallots, sliced

4 slices bacon, chopped
8 juniper berries
4 tablespoons port
$^2/_3$ cup red wine
2 tablespoons butter
2 tablespoons walnut oil

$^1/_4$ cup all-purpose flour
salt and pepper
new potatoes and green beans,
   to serve

1 Place the chicken in an ovenproof dish. Add the peppercorns, fresh cherries or canned cherries and their juice, if using, and the shallots.

2 Add the bacon, juniper berries, port, and red wine. Season well.

3 Place the chicken in the refrigerator and let marinate for 48 hours.

4 Heat the butter and walnut oil in a large skillet. Remove the chicken from the marinade and fry quickly in the skillet for 4 minutes on each side.

5 Return the chicken to the marinade, reserving the butter, oil, and juices in the pan.

6 Cover the dish with foil and bake in a preheated oven at 350°F for 20 minutes. Transfer the chicken to a large warm serving dish. Stir the flour into the juices in the skillet and cook over low heat, stirring, for 4 minutes. Add the marinade and bring to a boil, then simmer for 10 minutes, until the sauce thickens and reaches a smooth consistency.

7 Pour the cherry sauce over the chicken breasts and serve with new potatoes and green beans.

Scotch Whisky Roast Chicken

An unusual change from a plain roast, with a distinctly warming Scottish flavor and a delicious oatmeal stuffing.

Serves 6

INGREDIENTS

1 chicken, weighing 4½ pounds
oil, for brushing
1 tablespoon heather honey
2 tablespoons Scotch whisky
2 tablespoons all-purpose flour
1¼ cups chicken stock

STUFFING:
1 medium onion, finely chopped
1 stalk celery, thinly sliced
1 tablespoon butter or sunflower oil
1 teaspoon dried thyme
4 tablespoons rolled oats
4 tablespoons chicken stock

salt and pepper
a green vegetable and sautéed
    potatoes, to serve

1 First make the stuffing. Heat the butter or oil in a small saucepan. Add the onion and celery and fry, stirring constantly, over moderate heat until softened and lightly browned.

2 Remove from the heat and stir in the thyme, oats, stock, salt, and pepper.

3 Stuff the neck end of the chicken with the mixture and tuck the neck flap under. Place in a roasting pan, brush lightly with oil, and roast in a preheated oven at 375°F for about 1 hour.

4 Mix the heather honey with 1 tablespoon whisky and brush the mixture over the chicken. Return to the oven for a further 20 minutes, or until the chicken is golden brown and the juices run clear when the chicken is pierced through the thickest part with the point of a sharp knife.

5 Lift the chicken onto a serving plate. Skim the fat from the juices, then stir in the flour. Stir over moderate heat until the mixture starts to bubble, then gradually add the stock and remaining whisky.

6 Bring to a boil, stirring, then simmer for 1 minute. Serve the chicken with the whisky sauce, a green vegetable, and sautéed potatoes.

Roast Chicken in Exotic Mushroom Sauce

This unusual chicken dish has the flavor of roast chicken, but is finished off in a casserole with an exotic mushroom sauce.

Serves 4

INGREDIENTS

¹/₃ cup butter, softened
1 garlic clove, crushed
1 large chicken
2¹/₄ cups exotic mushrooms
1–2 shallots
2 tablespoons all-purpose flour

²/₃ cup brandy
1¹/₄ cups heavy cream
salt and pepper
1 tablespoon chopped fresh
  parsley, to garnish

wild rice or roast potatoes and green
  beans, to serve

1 Place the butter, garlic, and salt and pepper in a bowl and combine well.

2 Rub the mixture inside and outside of the chicken and set aside for 2 hours.

3 Place the chicken in a large roasting pan and roast in the center of a preheated oven at 450°F for 1½ hours, basting with the garlic butter about every 10 minutes.

4 Remove the chicken from the roasting pan and set aside to cool slightly.

5 Transfer the chicken juices to a saucepan and cook the mushrooms and shallots for 5 minutes. Sprinkle with the flour. Add the warm brandy and ignite using a taper or long match.

6 Add the heavy cream and cook for 3 minutes on very low heat, stirring all the time.

7 Remove the bones and cut the chicken into small bite-size pieces, then place the meat in a casserole dish. Cover with the mushroom sauce and bake in the oven, with the temperature reduced to 325°F for a further 12 minutes. Garnish with the parsley and serve with wild rice or roast potatoes and green beans.

Honeyed Citrus Chicken

This fat-free recipe is great for summer entertaining served simply with salad greens and new potatoes. If you cut the chicken in half and press it flat, you can roast it in under an hour.

Serves 4

INGREDIENTS

1 chicken, weighing 4^1/$_2$ pounds
salt and pepper
tarragon sprigs, to garnish

MARINADE:
1^1/$_4$ cups orange juice
3 tablespoons cider vinegar
3 tablespoons clear honey

2 tablespoons chopped
  fresh tarragon
2 oranges, cut into wedges

SAUCE:
handful of tarragon sprigs, chopped
1 cup fat-free ricotta cheese or
  strained plain yogurt

2 tablespoons orange juice
1 teaspoon clear honey
^{1}/$_2$ cup stuffed olives, chopped

1 Put the chicken on a chopping board with the breast downward. Cut through the bottom part of the carcass using poultry shears or heavy kitchen scissors, making sure not to cut right through to the breast bone below.

2 Rinse the chicken with cold water, drain, and place on a board with the skin side uppermost. Press the chicken flat, then cut off the leg ends.

3 Thread two long wooden skewers through the bird to keep it flat. Season the skin.

4 Put all the marinade ingredients, except the orange wedges, in a shallow, nonmetallic dish. Mix, then add the chicken. Cover and chill for 4 hours, turning the chicken several times.

5 To make the sauce, mix all the ingredients and season. Spoon into a serving dish, cover and chill.

6 Transfer the chicken and marinade to a roasting pan, open out the chicken and place skin side downward. Tuck the orange wedges around the chicken and roast in a preheated oven at 400°F for 25 minutes. Turn the chicken over and roast for another 20–30 minutes. Baste until the chicken is browned and the juices run clear when the thickest part is pierced with the point of a sharp knife. Garnish with tarragon and serve with the sauce.

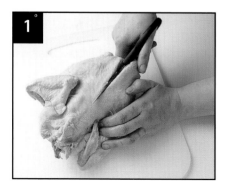

Breast of Chicken with Smoked Ham & Stilton Cheese

Beets are one of the most underrated vegetables, adding flavor and color to numerous dishes. Tender young beets are used in this recipe.

Serves 4

INGREDIENTS

4 chicken breasts
8 fresh sage leaves
8 thin slices of smoked ham
2 cups Stilton cheese,
 cut into 8 slices

8 slices bacon
2/3 cup chicken stock
2 tablespoons port
24 baby onions
1 pound 2 ounces baby beets, cooked

1 tablespoon cornstarch, blended
 with a little port to make a paste
salt and pepper

1 Cut a long slit horizontally along each chicken breast to make a pocket.

2 Insert 2 sage leaves into each pocket and season lightly.

3 Wrap each slice of ham around a slice of cheese and place 2 into each chicken pocket. Carefully wrap enough bacon around each breast completely to cover the pockets containing the ham and the cheese.

4 Place the breasts in an ovenproof dish and pour over the stock and port.

5 Add the baby onions, cover with a lid or cooking foil, and braise in a preheated oven at 375°F for about 40 minutes.

6 Carefully place each breast on a cutting board and slice through them to create a fan effect. Serve them on a warm serving dish with the baby onions and beets.

7 Put the juices from the casserole into a saucepan and bring to a boil, remove from the heat, and add the cornstarch paste. Gently simmer and cook the sauce for 2 minutes, then pour over the baby onions and beets.

VARIATION

Use any blue-veined cheese instead of the Stilton, if desired. Try Gorgonzola or Roquefort.

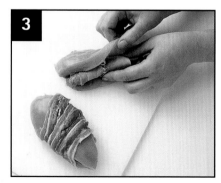

Springtime Roast Cornish Hens

Rock Cornish hens are simple to prepare, take about 30 minutes to roast, and can be easily cut in half lengthwise with a sharp knife. One hen makes a substantial serving for each person.

Serves 4

INGREDIENTS

5 tablespoons fresh brown
    bread crumbs
$1/2$ cup reduced fat crème fraîche
5 tablespoons chopped fresh parsley
5 tablespoons chopped fresh chives
4 rock Cornish hens
1 tablespoon sunflower oil

$1^1/2$ pounds young spring
    vegetables, such as carrots,
    zucchini, sugar snap
    peas, corn, and turnips, cut into
    small chunks
$1/2$ cup boiling chicken stock
2 teaspoons cornstarch

$2/3$ cup dry white wine
salt and pepper

1 In a bowl, mix together the bread crumbs, one third of the reduced fat crème fraîche, and 2 tablespoons each of parsley and chives. Season well with salt and pepper, then spoon into the neck ends of the rock Cornish hens. Place the rock Cornish hens on a rack in a roasting pan, brush with oil, and season well.

2 Roast in a preheated oven at 425°F for 30–35 minutes, or until the juices run clear, not pink, when the birds are pierced with the point of a sharp knife.

3 Place the vegetables in a shallow ovenproof dish in one layer and add half the remaining herbs, together with the chicken stock. Cover and bake for 25–30 minutes, until tender. Strain the vegetables, reserving the cooking juices, and keep warm.

4 Lift the rock Cornish hens onto a large, warm serving plate and skim any fat from the juices in the pan. Add the reserved vegetable juices.

5 Blend the cornstarch with the wine and whisk into the sauce with the remaining reduced fat crème fraîche. Whisk over moderate heat until the sauce is boiling, then add the remaining herbs. Season to taste with salt and pepper. Spoon the sauce over the rock Cornish hens and serve at once with the vegetables.

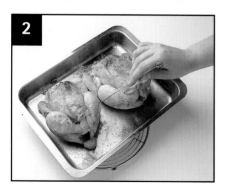

Boned Chicken with Parmesan

*It's really very easy to bone a whole chicken, but if you prefer,
you can ask a friendly butcher to do this for you.*

Serves 6

INGREDIENTS

1 chicken, weighing
   about 5 pounds
8 slices mortadella or salami
2 cups fresh white
   or brown bread crumbs

1 cup freshly grated
   Parmesan cheese
2 garlic cloves, crushed
6 tablespoons chopped fresh basil
   or parsley

1 egg, beaten
pepper
fresh spring vegetables, to serve

1   Bone the chicken, keeping the skin intact. Dislocate each leg by breaking it at the thigh joint. Cut down each side of the backbone, taking care not to pierce the breast skin.

2   Pull the backbone clear of the flesh and discard. Remove the ribs, severing any attached flesh with a sharp knife.

3   Scrape the flesh from each leg and cut away the bone at the joint with a knife or shears.

4   Use the bones for stock. Lay out the boned chicken on a board, skin side down. Arrange the mortadella slices over the chicken, overlapping slightly.

5   Put the bread crumbs, Parmesan cheese, garlic, and basil or parsley in a bowl. Season well with pepper and mix. Stir in the beaten egg to bind the mixture together. Pile the mixture down the middle of the boned chicken, roll the meat around it, and tie securely with fine cotton string.

6   Place in a roasting pan and brush lightly with olive oil. Roast in a preheated oven at 400°F for 1½ hours, or until the juices run clear when the chicken is pierced with a sharp knife.

7   Serve hot or cold, in slices, with fresh spring vegetables.

VARIATION

*Replace the mortadella with slices of
bacon, if desired.*

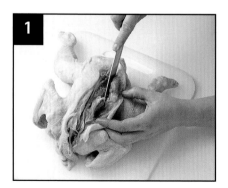

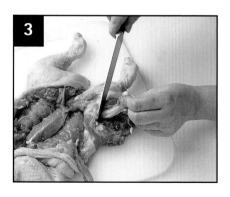

Chicken with Creamy Zucchini & Lime Stuffing

A cheese stuffing is tucked under the breast skin of the chicken to give added flavor and moistness to the meat.

Serves 6

INGREDIENTS

1 chicken, weighing 5 pounds
oil for brushing
1 1/3 cups zucchini
2 tablespoons butter
juice of 1 lime

STUFFING:
1/2 cup zucchini
3/4 cup medium-fat
  soft cheese
finely grated rind of
  1 lime

2 tablespoons fresh
  bread crumbs
salt and pepper

1 To make the stuffing, trim and coarsely grate the zucchini and mix with the cheese, lime rind, bread crumbs, salt, and pepper.

2 Carefully ease the skin away from the breast of the chicken.

3 Push the stuffing under the skin with your fingers to cover the breast evenly.

4 Place the chicken in a baking pan, brush with oil, and roast in a preheated oven at 375°F for 1 1/2–2 hours, or until the juices run clear when the thickest part of the chicken is pierced with the point of a sharp knife.

5 Meanwhile, trim the remaining zucchini and cut into long, thin strips with a vegetable peeler or sharp knife. Sauté in the butter and lime juice until just tender, then serve with the chicken.

COOK'S TIP

For quicker cooking, finely grate the zucchini, rather than cutting them into strips.

Pot Roast Orange & Sesame Chicken

This colorful, nutritious pot roast could be served for a family meal or for a special dinner.
Add more vegetables if you're feeding a crowd—if your roasting pot is large enough!

Serves 4

INGREDIENTS

2 tablespoons sunflower oil
1 chicken, weighing about
   3 pounds 5 ounces
2 large oranges
2 small onions, quartered

2 cups small whole
   carrots or thin carrots, cut
   into 2-inch lengths
$^2/_3$ cup orange juice
2 tablespoons brandy

2 tablespoons sesame seeds
1 tablespoon cornstarch
salt and pepper

1 Heat the oil in a large flameproof casserole and fry the chicken, turning occasionally, until evenly browned.

2 Cut one orange in half and place half inside the chicken cavity. Place the chicken in a large, deep casserole. Arrange the onions and carrots around the chicken.

3 Season well and pour in the orange juice.

4 Cut the remaining oranges into thin wedges and tuck them around the chicken in the casserole, among the vegetables.

5 Cover and cook in a preheated oven at 350°F for about 1½ hours, or until there is no trace of pink in the chicken juices when it is pierced, and the vegetables are tender. Remove the lid, sprinkle the chicken with the brandy and sesame seeds, and return to the oven for 10 minutes.

6 To serve, lift the chicken onto a large platter. Place the vegetables around the chicken.

Skim any excess fat from the juices. Blend the cornstarch with 1 tablespoon cold water, then stir into the juices, and bring to a boil, stirring all the time. Adjust the seasoning to taste, then serve the sauce with the chicken.

VARIATION

Use lemons instead of oranges for a sharper citrus flavor and place a sprig of fresh thyme in the chicken cavity with the lemon half, as they are a good flavor combination.

Honey & Mustard Baked Chicken

Chicken pieces are brushed with a classic combination of honey and mustard, then a crunchy coating of poppy seeds is added.

Serves 4–6

INGREDIENTS

8 chicken pieces
4 tablespoons butter, melted
4 tablespoons mild mustard
4 tablespoons clear honey
2 tablespoons lemon juice
1 teaspoon paprika

3 tablespoons poppy seeds
salt and pepper
tomato and corn salad,
  to serve

1 Place the chicken pieces, skinless side down, on a large cookie sheet.

2 Place all the ingredients, except the poppy seeds, into a large bowl and blend together thoroughly.

3 Brush the mixture over the chicken portions.

4 Bake in the center of a preheated oven at 400°F for 15 minutes.

5 Carefully turn over the chicken pieces and coat the top side of the chicken with the remaining honey and mustard mixture.

6 Sprinkle the chicken with poppy seeds and return to the oven for a further 15 minutes.

7 Arrange the chicken on a large, warm serving dish, pour over the cooking juices, and serve with a tomato and corn salad, if desired.

COOK'S TIP

Mexican rice makes an excellent accompaniment to this dish: boil the rice for 10 minutes, drain, then fry for 5 minutes. Add chopped onions, garlic, tomatoes, carrots, and chili and cook for 1 minute before adding stock. Bring to a boil, cover, and simmer for 20 minutes, adding more stock if necessary. Add peas 5 minutes before the end of the cooking time.

Mediterranean-Style Sunday Roast

A roast that is full of Mediterranean flavor. A mixture of feta cheese, rosemary, and sun-dried tomatoes is stuffed under the chicken skin, then roasted with garlic, new potatoes, and vegetables.

Serves 6

INGREDIENTS

1 chicken, weighing 5¹/₂ pounds
sprigs of fresh rosemary
³/₄ cup coarsely grated
    feta cheese
2 tablespoons sun-dried
    tomato paste

4 tablespoons butter, softened
1 bulb garlic
2¹/₄ pounds new potatoes, halved
    if large
1 each red, green, and yellow
    bell peppers, cut into chunks

3 zucchini, thinly sliced
2 tablespoons olive oil
2 tablespoons all-purpose flour
2¹/₂ cups chicken stock
salt and pepper

1 Rinse the chicken inside and out with cold water and drain well. Carefully cut between the skin and the top of the breast meat using a small pointed knife. Slide a finger into the slit and carefully enlarge it to form a pocket. Continue until the skin is completely lifted away from both breasts and the top of the legs.

2 Chop the leaves from 3 rosemary stems. Mix with the feta, sun-dried tomato paste, butter, and pepper, then spoon under the skin. Put the chicken in a large roasting pan, cover loosely with foil, and cook in a preheated oven at 375°F for 1¹/₂–2 hours or until the juices run clear, not pink, when the skin is pierced.

3 Break the garlic bulb into cloves, but do not peel. Add the vegetables to the chicken after 40 minutes.

4 Drizzle with oil, tuck in a few stems of rosemary, and season well. Cook for the remaining time, removing the foil for the last 40 minutes to brown the chicken.

5 Transfer the chicken to a serving platter. Place some of the vegetables around the chicken and transfer the remainder to a warm serving dish. Pour the fat out of the roasting pan and stir the flour into the remaining pan juices. Cook for 2 minutes, then gradually stir in the stock. Bring to a boil, stirring until thickened. Strain into a sauce boat and serve with the chicken.

Cheddar Baked Chicken

Cheese and mustard, and a simple, crispy coating, make a delicious combination for this healthy dish.

Serves 4

INGREDIENTS

1 tablespoon milk

2 tablespoons prepared
English mustard

1 cup grated sharp cheddar cheese

3 tablespoons all-purpose flour

2 tablespoons chopped fresh chives

4 skinless, boneless chicken breasts

1 Mix together the milk and mustard in a bowl. In another bowl, combine the cheese, flour, and chives.

2 Dip the chicken into the milk and mustard mixture, brushing to coat evenly.

3 Dip the chicken breasts into the cheese mixture, pressing to coat evenly. Place on a cookie sheet and spoon any spare cheese coating over the top.

4 Bake in a preheated oven at 400°F for 30–35 minutes, or until golden brown and the juices run clear, not pink, when it is pierced with the point of a sharp knife. Serve hot, with baked potatoes and fresh vegetables, or serve cold, with a crisp salad.

COOK'S TIP

There are several varieties of mustard available. For a sharper flavor try French varieties—Meaux mustard has a grainy texture with a warm, spicy flavor, while Dijon mustard is medium-hot and tangy.

COOK'S TIP

It is a good idea to freeze herbs, as they retain their color, flavor, and nutrients very well. Chives are particularly suitable for freezing— store them in labeled plastic bags and shake them dry before use. Dried chives are not an adequate substitute for fresh.

Gardener's Chicken

Any combination of small, young vegetables can be roasted with the chicken, such as zucchini, leeks, and onions.

Serves 4

INGREDIENTS

4 cups peeled and chopped parsnips
3/4 cup peeled and chopped carrots
1/2 cup fresh bread crumbs
1/4 teaspoon grated nutmeg
1 tablespoon chopped fresh parsley

1 chicken, weighing 3 pounds
  5 ounces
bunch parsley
1/2 onion
2 tablespoons butter, softened
4 tablespoons olive oil

1 pound 2 ounces new potatoes,
  scrubbed
1 pound 2 ounces baby carrots
  washed and trimmed
salt and pepper
chopped fresh parsley, to garnish

1 To make the stuffing, put the parsnips and carrots into a pan, half cover with water, and bring to a boil. Cover the pan and simmer until tender. Drain well, then purée in a blender or food processor. Transfer the purée to a bowl and set aside to cool.

2 Mix in the bread crumbs, nutmeg, and parsley and season with salt and pepper.

3 Put the stuffing into the neck end of the chicken and push a

little under the skin over the breast meat. Secure the flap of skin with a small metal skewer or toothpick.

4 Place the bunch of parsley and onion inside the cavity of the chicken, then place the chicken in a large roasting pan.

5 Spread the butter over the skin and season with salt and pepper, cover with foil, and cook in a preheated oven at 375°F for 30 minutes.

6 Meanwhile, heat the oil in a skillet and lightly brown the potatoes.

7 Transfer the potatoes to the roasting pan and add the baby carrots. Baste the chicken and continue to cook for 1 further hour, basting the chicken and vegetables after 30 minutes. Remove the foil for the last 20 minutes to allow the skin to crispen. Garnish the vegetables with chopped parsley and serve at once.

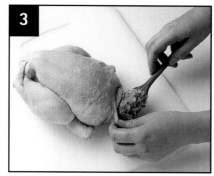

Barbecues & Broils

There is nothing more delicious than the juicy flesh and charred skin of chicken that has been broiled over an open fire—after marinating in a flavorful mixture of oil and herbs or spices. Try an Asian-style mixture of yogurt and aromatic spices, or soy sauce, sesame oil, and fresh ginger root. There are some unusual flavors and innovative tastes, including Skewered Chicken with Blackberry Sauce, and Skewered Chicken Spirals, which are attractive whirls of chicken, bacon, and basil. Rock Cornish hens, flavored with lemon and tarragon in this section, are perfect for broiling or barbecuing. There is also a recipe for Broiled Chicken Salad, which combines chicken breasts with a selection of broiled vegetables, including zucchini, eggplant, and red bell pepper drizzled with olive oil and served with crusty bread to soak up the delicious juices.

Chicken Cajun-Style

These spicy chicken wings are good served with a chili salsa and salad. Alternatively, if this is too spicy for your taste, try a sour cream and chive dip.

Serves 4

INGREDIENTS

16 chicken wings
4 teaspoons paprika
2 teaspoons ground coriander
1 teaspoon celery salt
1 teaspoon ground cumin
$1/2$ teaspoon cayenne pepper

$1/2$ teaspoon salt
1 tablespoon oil
2 tablespoons red wine vinegar
fresh parsley, to garnish
cherry tomatoes and mixed salad
    greens, to serve

1 Wash the chicken wings and dry with absorbent paper towels. Remove the wing tips with kitchen scissors.

2 Mix together the paprika, coriander, celery salt, cumin, cayenne pepper, the salt, oil, and red wine vinegar.

3 Rub this mixture over the wings to coat evenly and set aside, in the refrigerator for at least 1 hour to allow the flavors to permeate the chicken.

4 Cook the wings on a preheated barbecue, occasionally brushing with oil, for about 15 minutes, turning often, until cooked through. Garnish with fresh parsley and serve with cherry tomatoes, mixed salad greens, and a sauce of your choice.

COOK'S TIP

To save time, you can buy ready-made Cajun spice seasoning to rub over the chicken wings.

VARIATION

Although chicken wings do not have much meat on them, they are small and easy to pick up, which makes them ideal for barbecues. However, they can also be enjoyed fried or roasted.

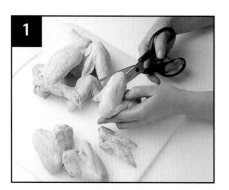

Spicy Sesame Chicken

This is a quick-and-easy recipe for the broiler, perfect for lunch or to eat outdoors on a picnic.

Serves 4

INGREDIENTS

4 chicken quarters
$1/2$ cup plain yogurt

finely grated rind and juice
of 1 small lemon
2 teaspoons medium-hot curry paste

1 tablespoon sesame seeds
lemon wedges, to garnish
salad and nan bread, to serve

1 Remove the skin from the chicken and make cuts in the flesh at intervals with a sharp knife.

2 In a small bowl, thoroughly combine the plain yogurt, lemon rind, lemon juice, and curry paste to form a smooth mixture.

3 Spoon the mixture over the chicken quarters and arrange them on a foil-lined broiler pan or cookie sheet.

4 Place the chicken quarters under a preheated broiler and broil for about 12–15 minutes, turning once. Broil until golden brown and thoroughly cooked. Just before the end of the cooking time, sprinkle the chicken with the sesame seeds.

5 Serve at once, garnished with lemon wedges, with a salad and nan bread.

COOK'S TIP

If you have time, leave the chicken and the sauce in the refrigerator to marinate overnight so the flavors are fully absorbed.

VARIATION

Poppy seeds, fennel seeds, or cumin seeds, or a mixture of all three, can also be used to sprinkle over the chicken.

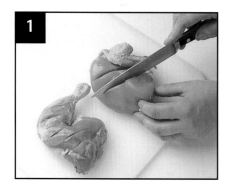

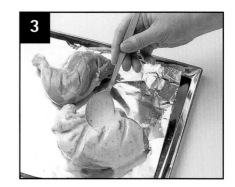

Ginger Chicken & Corn

Chicken wings and corn in a sticky ginger marinade are designed to be eaten with the fingers—there's no other way!

Serves 6

INGREDIENTS

3 fresh ears of corn
12 chicken wings
1-inch piece fresh ginger root

6 tablespoons lemon juice
4 teaspoons sunflower oil
1 tablespoon golden superfine sugar

baked potatoes or salad,
to serve

1 Remove the husks and silken hairs from the corn. Using a sharp knife, cut each cob into 6 slices. Place in a large bowl with the chicken wings.

2 Peel and grate the ginger root or chop finely.

3 Mix the ginger root with the lemon juice, sunflower oil, and golden superfine sugar, then toss with the corn and chicken to coat.

4 Thread the corn and chicken wings onto skewers, to make turning easier.

5 Cook the corn and chicken under a preheated broiler or on a barbecue for about 15–20 minutes, basting with the gingery glaze and turning frequently, until the corn is golden brown and tender and the chicken is cooked through. Serve at once with baked potatoes or salad.

COOK'S TIP

Cut off the wing tips before broiling, as they burn very easily. Alternatively, you can cover them with small pieces of foil.

COOK'S TIP

When you are buying fresh corn, look for plump, tightly packed kernels. If fresh corn is unavailable, you can use thawed, frozen corn instead.

Broiled Chicken & Vegetable Salad

Broiling is a quick, healthy cooking method, ideal for sealing in the juices and flavor of chicken breasts, and a wonderful way to cook summer vegetables.

Serves 4

INGREDIENTS

1 small eggplant, sliced
2 garlic cloves, crushed
finely grated rind of $^1/_2$ lemon
1 tablespoon chopped fresh mint
6 tablespoons olive oil
4 boneless chicken breasts

2 medium zucchini, sliced
1 medium red bell
  pepper, quartered
1 small bulb fennel, sliced thickly
1 large red onion, sliced thickly

1 small Italian loaf or
  1 French baguette, sliced
extra olive oil
salt and pepper

1 Place the eggplant slices in a colander and sprinkle with salt. Leave over a bowl to drain for 30 minutes, then rinse, and dry. This will get rid of the bitter juices.

2 Mix together the garlic, lemon rind, mint, and olive oil and season.

3 Slash the chicken breasts at intervals with a sharp knife.

Stir the oil mixture to combine and spoon half over the chicken breasts.

4 In a separate bowl, combine the eggplants and the remaining vegetables, then toss in the remaining oil mixture. Set the chicken and vegetables aside to marinate for about 30 minutes.

5 Place the chicken breasts and vegetables on a preheated hot broiler or barbecue, turning

occasionally, until they are golden brown and tender. Alternatively, cook on a ridged griddle pan on the stove.

6 Brush the bread slices with olive oil and broil until they are golden.

7 Drizzle a little olive oil over the chicken and broiled vegetables and serve hot or cold with the crusty bread toasts.

Tropical Chicken Skewers

In this recipe, chicken is given a Caribbean flavor. The marinade keeps them moist and succulent during cooking.

Serves 6

INGREDIENTS

1 pound 10 ounces boneless
   chicken breasts
2 tablespoons medium sherry

3 mangoes
bay leaves
2 tablespoons oil

2 tablespoons coarsely
   shredded coconut
pepper

1 Remove the skin from the chicken, cut the flesh into 1-inch cubes, and toss in the sherry, together with a little pepper, coating them well.

2 Using a sharp knife, cut the mango into wedges. Peel and cut the wedges into 1-inch cubes.

3 Thread the chicken, mango cubes, and bay leaves alternately onto long skewers, then brush lightly with oil.

4 Broil the skewers on a preheated broiler for about 8–10 minutes, turning occasionally, until golden.

5 Sprinkle the skewers with the coconut and broil for a further 30 seconds. Serve with a crisp salad.

COOK'S TIP

Use mangoes that are ripe, but still firm so that they hold together on the skewers during cooking. Another firm fruit that would be suitable is pineapple.

COOK'S TIP

Remember that if you are using metal skewers, they will get very hot, so be sure to use potholders or tongs to turn them. Wooden skewers should be soaked in water for 30 minutes before use to prevent them from burning on the barbecue, and the exposed ends should be covered with pieces of kitchen foil.

Sweet & Sour Drumsticks

Chicken drumsticks are marinated to impart a tangy, sweet-and-sour flavor and a shiny glaze.

Serves 4

INGREDIENTS

8 chicken drumsticks
4 tablespoons red wine vinegar
2 tablespoons tomato paste
2 tablespoons soy sauce

2 tablespoons clear honey
1 tablespoon Worcestershire sauce
1 garlic clove
good pinch of cayenne pepper

salt and pepper
sprig of fresh parsley, to garnish
salad, to serve

1 Skin the chicken, if desired, and slash the flesh 2–3 times with a sharp knife.

2 Lay the chicken drumsticks side by side in a shallow nonmetallic container.

3 Mix the red wine vinegar, tomato paste, soy sauce, honey, Worcestershire sauce, garlic, and cayenne pepper together and pour over the chicken drumsticks.

4 Marinate in the refrigerator for 1 hour. Cook the drumsticks on a preheated barbecue for about 20 minutes, brushing frequently with the marinade and turning during cooking. Garnish with parsley and serve with a crisp salad.

COOK'S TIP

For a tangy flavor, add the juice of 1 lime to the marinade. While the drumsticks are cooking, check regularly to ensure that they are not burning.

VARIATION

This sweet-and-sour marinade would also work well with pork or shrimp. Thread pork cubes or shrimp onto skewers with bell peppers and pearl onions.

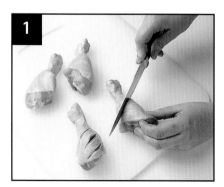

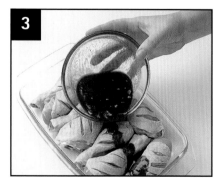

Chicken with Garden Herbs

Warm weather calls for lighter eating, and this chilled chicken dish in a subtle herb vinaigrette is ideal for a summer dinner party, or for a picnic.

Serves 4

INGREDIENTS

4 skinless, boneless chicken breasts
6 tablespoons olive oil
2 tablespoons lemon juice

4 tablespoons finely chopped
   summer herbs, such as parsley,
   chives, and mint
1 ripe avocado

$1/2$ cup ricotta cheese or strained
   unsweetened yogurt
pepper
cold rice, to serve

1 Using a sharp knife, cut 3–4 deep slashes in the chicken breasts.

2 Place in a flameproof dish and brush lightly with a little of the olive oil.

3 Cook the chicken on a preheated broiler, turning once, until golden and the juices run clear when the chicken is pierced in the thickest part with the point of a sharp knife.

4 Combine the remaining oil with the lemon juice and herbs and season with pepper. Spoon the oil over the chicken and set aside to cool. Chill in the refrigerator for at least 1 hour.

5 Mash the avocado or purée in a food processor with the ricotta cheese or yogurt. Season with pepper. Serve the chicken with the avocado sauce and rice.

COOK'S TIP

The chicken can be cooked several hours before you need it and stored in the refrigerator until required.

COOK'S TIP

To remove the pit easily from an avocado, first cut the avocado in half. Holding one half securely in your hand, rap the knife into the pit so that it becomes embedded in the pit, then carefully twist the knife to dislodge the pit.

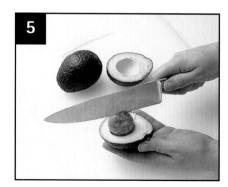

Skewered Spicy Tomato Chicken

These low-fat, spicy skewers are cooked in a matter of minutes—and they can be assembled ahead of time and stored in the refrigerator until you need them.

Serves 4

INGREDIENTS

1 pound 2 ounces skinless, boneless chicken breasts
3 tablespoons tomato paste
2 tablespoons clear honey

2 tablespoons Worcestershire sauce
1 tablespoon chopped fresh rosemary
9 ounces cherry tomatoes

sprigs of rosemary, to garnish
couscous or rice, to serve

1 Using a sharp knife, cut the chicken into 1-inch chunks and place in a bowl.

2 Mix together the tomato paste, honey, Worcestershire sauce, and rosemary. Add to the chicken, stirring to coat evenly and thoroughly.

3 Alternating the chicken pieces and tomatoes, thread them onto eight wooden skewers.

4 Spoon over any remaining glaze. Cook under a preheated broiler for about

8–10 minutes, turning occasionally, until the chicken is thoroughly cooked. Serve on a bed of couscous or rice and garnish with sprigs of rosemary.

COOK'S TIP

Couscous is made from semolina that has been made into separate grains. It is very easy to prepare—simply soak it in a bowl of boiling water and then fluff up the grains with a fork. Flavorings, such as lemon or nutmeg, can be added.

COOK'S TIP

Cherry tomatoes are ideal for barbecues as they can be threaded straight onto skewers. As they are kept whole, the skins keep in the tomatoes natural juices.

Broiled Chicken with Pesto Toasts

This Italian-style dish is richly flavored with pesto, which is a mixture of basil, olive oil, pine nuts, and Parmesan cheese. Either red or green pesto can be used for this recipe.

Serves 4

INGREDIENTS

8 part-boned chicken thighs
olive oil, for brushing
$1^2/_3$ cups sieved tomatoes
$^1/_2$ cup green or red
   pesto sauce

12 slices French bread
1 cup freshly grated
   Parmesan cheese
$^1/_2$ cup pine nuts
   or slivered almonds

basil sprig, to garnish

1 Put the chicken in a single layer in a wide flameproof dish and brush with oil. Place under a preheated broiler for about 15 minutes, turning occasionally, until golden brown.

2 Pierce the thighs with the point of a sharp knife to ensure that the there is no trace of pink in the juices.

3 Pour off any excess fat. Warm the sieved tomatoes and half the pesto sauce in a small saucepan and pour over the chicken. Broil for a few more minutes, turning until coated.

4 Meanwhile, spread the remaining pesto onto the slices of bread. Arrange the bread over the chicken and sprinkle with the Parmesan cheese. Scatter the pine nuts over the cheese. Broil for 2–3 minutes, until browned and bubbling. Serve hot, garnished with a basil sprig.

COOK'S TIP

Leaving the skin on means the chicken will have a higher fat content, but many people like the rich taste and crispy skin, especially when it is blackened by the barbecue. The skin also keeps in the cooking juices.

Mustardy Barbecued Drumsticks

Great for barbecues, or for simple summer lunches and picnics,
this is an easy and tasty recipe for chicken drumsticks.

Serves 4

INGREDIENTS

10 slices smoked bacon
1 garlic clove, peeled
  and crushed
3 tablespoons whole-grain mustard

4 tablespoons fresh brown
  bread crumbs
8 chicken drumsticks

1 tablespoon sunflower oil
fresh parsley sprigs, to garnish

1 Chop two of the bacon slices into small pieces and fry without additional fat for 3–4 minutes, stirring so that the bacon does not stick to the base of the pan. Remove from the heat and stir in the crushed garlic, 2 tablespoons of the whole-grain mustard, and the bread crumbs.

2 Carefully loosen the skin from each drumstick with your fingers, being careful not to tear the skin. Spoon a little of the mustard stuffing under each flap of skin, smoothing the skins over firmly afterward.

3 Wrap a bacon slice around each drumstick and secure with toothpicks.

4 Mix together the remaining mustard and the oil, brush over the chicken drumsticks, and cook on a barbecue or under a preheated broiler for about 25 minutes, until there is no trace of pink in the juices when the thickest part of the chicken is pierced with the point of a knife.

5 Garnish with the parsley sprigs. The drumsticks may be served hot or cold.

COOK'S TIP

Don't cook the chicken over the hottest part of the barbecue or the outside may be charred before the center is cooked.

Minty Lime Chicken

These tangy lime- and honey-coated pieces have a matching sauce or dip based on creamy yogurt.
They could be served at a barbecue or as a main course for a dinner party.

Serves 6

INGREDIENTS

3 tablespoons finely chopped mint
4 tablespoons clear honey
4 tablespoons lime juice
12 boneless chicken thighs
salad, to serve

SAUCE:
$^1/_2$ cup plain thick yogurt
1 tablespoon finely chopped mint
2 teaspoons finely grated lime rind

1 Combine the mint, honey, and lime juice in a bowl.

2 Use toothpicks to keep the chicken thighs in neat shapes and add the chicken to the marinade, turning to coat evenly.

3 Leave to marinate for at least 30 minutes, preferably overnight. Cook the chicken on a moderately hot barbecue or under a preheated broiler, turning frequently and basting with the marinade. The chicken is cooked if the juices run clear when the chicken is pierced in the thickest part with the point of a knife.

4 Meanwhile, mix together the sauce ingredients.

5 Remove the toothpicks and serve the chicken with a salad and the sauce.

VARIATION

Use this marinade for chicken kabobs, alternating the chicken with lime and red onion wedges.

COOK'S TIP

Mint can be grown very easily in a garden or window box. It is a useful herb for marinades and salad dressings. Other useful herbs to grow are parsley and basil.

Skewered Chicken with Blackberry Sauce

This fall recipe can be made with fresh blackberries
if you're lucky enough to have a good supply.

Serves 4

INGREDIENTS

4 chicken breasts or 8 thighs
4 tablespoons dry white wine or cider
2 tablespoons chopped
   fresh rosemary
pepper

rosemary sprigs
   and blackberries, to garnish
salad greens, to serve

SAUCE:
2 cups blackberries
1 tablespoon cider vinegar
2 tablespoons red currant jelly
$1/4$ teaspoon grated nutmeg

1 Using a sharp knife, cut the chicken into 1-inch pieces and place in a bowl. Sprinkle it with the white wine and rosemary, and season well with pepper. Cover and set aside to marinate for at least an hour.

2 Drain the chicken pieces thoroughly, reserving the marinade, and thread the meat onto 8 metal or presoaked wooden skewers.

3 Cook on a preheated broiler for about 8–10 minutes, turning occasionally, until golden brown and evenly cooked through.

4 Meanwhile, to make the sauce, place the marinade in a pan with the blackberries and simmer gently until soft. Press the mixture though a strainer using the back of a spoon.

5 Return the blackberry purée to the pan, add the cider vinegar and red currant jelly, and bring to a boil. Boil uncovered until the sauce is reduced by about one third.

6 Spoon a little bramble sauce onto each plate and place a chicken skewer on top. Sprinkle with nutmeg and serve hot. Garnish with rosemary and blackberries and serve.

COOK'S TIP

If you use canned fruit,
omit the red currant jelly.

Broiled Rock Cornish Hens with Lemon & Tarragon

Butterflied rock Cornish hens are complemented by the delicate fragrance of lemon and tarragon and broiled.

Serves 2

INGREDIENTS

2 rock Cornish hens
4 sprigs fresh tarragon
1 teaspoon oil
2 tablespoons butter

rind of $^1/_2$ lemon
1 tablespoon lemon juice
1 garlic clove, crushed
salt and pepper

tarragon and orange slices,
 to garnish
new potatoes, to serve

1 Prepare the rock Cornish hens, turn them breast side down on a chopping board, and cut them through the backbones using kitchen scissors. Crush each bird gently to break the bones, so that they lie flat while cooking. Season each with salt.

2 Turn them over and insert a sprig of tarragon under the skin over each side of the breast.

3 Brush the rock Cornish hens with oil, using a pastry brush, and place under a preheated broiler about 5 inches from the heat. Broil for about 15 minutes, turning half way, until they are lightly browned.

4 Meanwhile, to make the glaze, melt the butter in a small saucepan, add the lemon rind, lemon juice, and garlic, and season with salt and pepper.

5 Brush the rock Cornish hens with the glaze and cook for a further 15 minutes, turning them once and brushing regularly so that they stay moist. Garnish the rock Cornish hens with tarragon and orange slices and serve with new potatoes.

COOK'S TIP

Once the rock Cornish hens are flattened, insert 2 metal skewers through them to keep them flat.

Barbecued Chicken Quarters with Warm Aïoli

Chicken quarters are barbecued, then served with a strongly flavored garlic mayonnaise, which originated in Provence, France.

Serves 4

INGREDIENTS

4 chicken quarters
2 tablespoons oil
2 tablespoons lemon juice
2 teaspoons dried thyme
salt and pepper

salad greens and lemon slices, to serve

AIOLI:
5 garlic cloves, crushed

2 egg yolks
$^1/_2$ cup olive oil
$^1/_2$ cup sunflower oil
2 teaspoons lemon juice
2 tablespoons boiling water

1 Using a skewer, prick the chicken quarters in several places, then place them in a shallow dish.

2 Combine the oil, lemon juice, thyme, and seasoning, then pour it over the chicken, turning to coat the chicken evenly. Set aside for 2 hours.

3 To make the aïoli, beat together the garlic and a pinch of salt to make a paste. Add the egg yolks and beat well.

Gradually add the oils, drop by drop, beating vigorously, until the mayonnaise becomes creamy and smooth. Add the oils in a thin steady trickle and continue beating until the aïoli is thick. Stir in the lemon juice and season with pepper. Set aside.

4 Place the chicken on a hot barbecue and cook for 25–30 minutes. Brush with the marinade and turn the portions to cook evenly. Remove and arrange on a serving plate.

5 Beat the water into the aïoli and turn into a warm serving bowl. Serve the barbecued chicken with the aïoli, salad greens, and lemon slices.

COOK'S TIP

To make a quick aïoli, add the garlic to $1^1/_4$ cups good-quality mayonnaise, then place in a bowl over a pan of warm water and beat together. Just before serving add 1–2 tablespoons hot water.

Skewered Chicken Spirals

These unusual chicken kebabs have a wonderful Mediterranean flavor, and the bacon helps keep them moist during cooking.

Serves 4

INGREDIENTS

4 skinless, boneless chicken breasts
1 garlic clove, crushed
2 tablespoons tomato paste

4 slices smoked bacon
large handful fresh basil leaves
oil for brushing

salt and pepper

1 Spread out a piece of chicken between two sheets of plastic wrap and beat firmly with a rolling pin or the flat side of a meat mallet to flatten the chicken to an even thickness. Repeat with the remaining pieces of chicken.

2 Mix together the crushed garlic and tomato paste until well blended. Spread the mixture evenly over the surface of the chicken.

3 Lay a bacon slice over each piece of chicken, then scatter with the fresh basil leaves. Season well with salt and pepper.

4 Roll up each piece of chicken firmly, then cut into thick slices using a sharp knife.

5 Thread the slices securely onto four skewers, making sure the skewer holds the chicken in a spiral shape.

6 Brush the skewers lightly with oil and cook on a hot barbecue or under a preheated broiler for about 5 minutes, then turn the skewers over, and cook for a further 5 minutes, until the chicken is cooked through. Serve the chicken spirals hot with salad greens.

COOK'S TIP

Flattening the chicken breasts makes them thinner, so that they cook more quickly. It also makes them easier to roll.

VARIATION

To complete the Mediterranean theme, serve these kebabs with Parmesan-topped garlic bread.

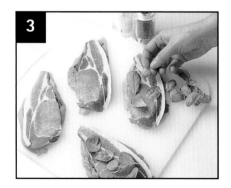

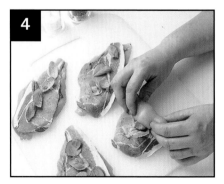

Spicy Dishes

Because chicken is popular throughout the world, there are countless spicy recipes from Asia, Mexico, the Caribbean, Spain, and Japan. Lime juice, peanut, coconut, and chile add the authentic tastes of Thailand to Chile Coconut Chicken, while Kashmiri Chicken is a rich and spicy dish from Northern India with an aromatic sauce made from yogurt, Tikka curry paste, cumin, ginger, chile, and almonds. From Spain comes Spanish Chicken with Shrimp, with its unusual mixture of chicken and shellfish, together with the famous spicy Spanish sausage, chorizo, slow-cooked in a sauce of garlic, tomatoes, and white wine. Cumin Spiced Apricot Chicken is a creative modern dish that would be perfect for any special occasion. The chicken is stuffed with dried apricots, coated in a yogurt, cumin, and turmeric sauce, and served with nutty rice. There is even a dish from Japan, Teppanyaki, a simple dish of fried chicken slices with bell peppers, scallions and bean sprouts, served with a Mirin dipping sauce.

Chicken in Red Bell Pepper & Almond Sauce

This tasty chicken dish combines warm spices and almonds and is spiked with anise.

Serves 4

INGREDIENTS

2 tablespoons butter

7 tablespoons vegetable oil

4 skinless, boneless chicken
   breasts, cut into
     2-inch x 1-inch pieces

1 medium onion, roughly chopped

1-inch piece fresh ginger root

3 garlic cloves, peeled

1/4 cup blanched almonds

1 large red bell pepper,
   roughly chopped

1 tablespoon ground cumin

2 teaspoons ground coriander

1 teaspoon ground turmeric

pinch of cayenne pepper

1/2 teaspoon salt

2/3 cup water

3 star anise

2 tablespoons lemon juice

pepper

slivered almonds,
   to garnish

rice, to serve

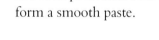

1 Heat the butter and 1 tablespoon of the oil in a skillet, add the chicken pieces, and cook for 5 minutes, until golden. Transfer the chicken pieces to a plate and keep warm until they are required.

2 Combine the onion, ginger, garlic, almonds, red bell pepper, cumin, coriander, turmeric, cayenne pepper, and salt in a food processor. Process to form a smooth paste.

3 Heat the remaining oil in a large saucepan or deep skillet. Add the spice paste and fry for 10–12 minutes.

4 Add the chicken pieces, the water, star anise, lemon juice, and pepper. Cover, reduce the heat, and simmer gently for 25 minutes, or until the chicken is tender, stirring a few times during cooking.

5 Transfer the chicken to a serving dish, sprinkle with the slivered almonds, and serve with individual rice moulds.

Fruity Garlic Curried Chicken

Serve this fruity curry with mango chutney and nan bread, and top the curry with seedless grapes. Mangoes or pears make a good substitute for pineapple.

Serves 4-6

INGREDIENTS

1 tablespoon oil
2 pounds chicken meat, chopped
4 tablespoons flour, seasoned
32 baby onions, roughly chopped
4 garlic cloves, crushed with a
    little olive oil
3 cooking apples, diced

1 pineapple, diced
3/4 cup golden raisins
1 tablespoon honey
1 1/4 cups chicken stock
2 tablespoons Worcestershire sauce
3 tablespoons hot curry paste
2/3 cup sour cream

salt and pepper
orange slices, to garnish
rice, to serve

1 Heat the oil in a large skillet. Coat the meat in the seasoned flour and cook for about 4 minutes, until it is browned all over. Transfer the chicken to a large deep casserole and keep warm until required.

2 Fry the onions, garlic, apples, pineapple, and golden raisins in the pan juices over low heat.

3 Add the honey, chicken stock, Worcestershire sauce, and hot curry paste. Season to taste with salt and pepper.

4 Pour the sauce over the chicken and cover the casserole with a lid or cooking foil.

5 Cook in the center of a preheated oven at 350°F for about 2 hours. Stir in the sour cream and cook for a further 15 minutes. Serve the curry at once with rice, garnished with a slice of orange.

VARIATION

Coconut rice also makes an excellent accompaniment to this dish. Place 1 ounce chopped creamed coconut, 1 cinnamon stick, and 2 1/4 cups water in a large saucepan and bring to a boil. Stir in 1 3/4 cups basmati rice, cover, and simmer gently for 15 minutes, until all the liquid has been absorbed. Remove and discard the cinnamon stick before serving.

Spicy Chicken Tortillas

Serve these easy-to-prepare tortillas to friends or as a special family supper.
The chicken filling has a mild, mellow spicy heat, and a fresh salad makes a perfect accompaniment.

Serves 4

INGREDIENTS

2 tablespoons oil

8 skinless, boneless chicken
  thighs, sliced

1 onion, chopped

2 garlic cloves, chopped

1 teaspoon cumin seeds,
  roughly crushed

2 large dried chiles, sliced

14 ounce can tomatoes

14 ounce can red kidney
  beans, drained

2/3 cup chicken stock

2 teaspoons sugar

salt and pepper

lime wedges, to garnish

TO SERVE:

1 large ripe avocado

1 lime

8 soft tortillas

1 cup thick yogurt

1 Heat the oil in a large skillet or wok, add the chicken and fry for 3 minutes, until golden. Add the onion and fry for 5 minutes, stirring until browned. Add the garlic, cumin, and chiles, with their seeds, and cook for about 1 minute.

2 Add the tomatoes, kidney beans, stock, sugar, and salt and pepper to taste. Bring to a boil, breaking up the tomatoes. Cover and simmer for 15 minutes.

Remove the lid and cook for 5 minutes, stirring occasionally, until the sauce has thickened.

3 Halve the avocado, discard the stone and scoop out the flesh onto a plate. Mash the avocado with a fork. Cut half of the lime into 8 thin wedges. Squeeze the juice from the remaining lime over the avocado.

4 Warm the tortillas following the instructions on the packet.

Put two tortillas on each serving plate, fill with the chicken mixture, and top with spoonfuls of avocado and yogurt. Garnish the tortillas with lime wedges.

VARIATION

For a vegetarian filling, replace the chicken with 14 ounces canned pinto or cannellini beans, and use vegetable stock instead of the chicken stock.

Cajun Chicken Gumbo

This complete main course is cooked in one saucepan for simplicity. If you're cooking for one, simply halve the ingredients; the cooking time should stay the same.

Serves 2

INGREDIENTS

1 tablespoon sunflower oil
4 chicken thighs
1 small onion, diced
2 stalks celery, diced

1 small green bell pepper, diced
$\frac{1}{2}$ cup long grain rice
$1\frac{1}{4}$ cups chicken stock
1 small red chile

9 ounces okra
1 tablespoon tomato paste
salt and pepper

1 Heat the oil in a wide pan and fry the chicken until golden. Remove the chicken from the pan using a slotted spoon. Stir in the onion, celery, and bell pepper and fry for 1 minute. Pour off any excess fat.

2 Add the rice and fry, stirring briskly, for a further minute. Add the chicken stock and heat until boiling.

3 Thinly slice the chile and trim the okra. Add to the pan, together with the tomato paste. Season to taste.

4 Return the chicken to the pan and stir. Cover tightly and simmer gently for 15 minutes, or until the rice is tender, the chicken is thoroughly cooked, and all the liquid absorbed. Stir occasionally and if the gumbo becomes too dry, add a little extra stock to moisten. Serve immediately.

COOK'S TIP

The whole chile makes the dish hot and spicy—if you prefer a milder flavor, discard the seeds of the chile.

VARIATION

You can replace the chicken with 9 ounces peeled shrimp and 3 ounces pork belly, if desired. Slice the pork and fry in the oil before adding the onions, and add the shrimp 5 minutes before the end of the cooking time.

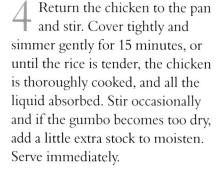

Mexican Chicken

*Chile, tomatoes, and corn are typical ingredients
in a Mexican dish.*

Serves 4

INGREDIENTS

2 tablespoons oil
8 chicken drumsticks
1 medium onion, finely chopped

1 teaspoon chile powder
1 teaspoon ground coriander
14 ounce can chopped tomatoes
2 tablespoons tomato paste
²/₃ cup frozen corn

salt and pepper
rice and mixed bell pepper salad,
   to serve

1 Heat the oil in a large skillet, add the chicken drumsticks, and cook over medium heat until lightly browned. Remove the chicken drumsticks from the skillet with a slotted spoon and set aside until required.

2 Add the chopped onion to the skillet and cook for 3–4 minutes, until softened, then stir in the chile powder and coriander, and cook for a few seconds, stirring briskly so the spices do not burn on the base of the skillet. Add the chopped tomatoes together with their can juice and the tomato paste and stir well to incorporate.

3 Return the chicken drumsticks to the skillet and simmer the casserole gently for 20 minutes, until the chicken is tender and thoroughly cooked. Add the corn and cook for a further 3–4 minutes. Season with salt and pepper to taste.

4 Serve the Mexican Chicken with rice and mixed bell pepper salad.

COOK'S TIP

Mexican dishes are not usually suitable for freezing because the strong flavors they contain, such as chile, intensify during freezing, and if left for too long, an unpleasant, musty flavor can develop.

Chicken with Bell Peppers & Black Bean Sauce

This tasty chicken stir-fry is quick and easy to make and is full of fresh flavors and crunchy vegetables.

Serves 4

INGREDIENTS

14 ounces chicken breasts,
   thinly sliced
pinch of cornstarch
2 tablespoons oil
1 garlic clove, crushed
1 tablespoon black bean sauce
1 small red bell pepper, cut into strips
1 small green bell pepper, cut
   into strips

1 red chile, finely chopped
1 cup sliced mushrooms
1 onion, chopped
6 scallions, chopped
salt and pepper
fresh noodles, to serve

SEASONING:
$^1/_2$ teaspoon salt
$^1/_2$ teaspoon sugar
3 tablespoons chicken stock
1 tablespoon dark soy sauce
2 tablespoons beef stock
2 tablespoons rice wine
1 teaspoon cornstarch, blended with
   a little rice wine

1 Put the chicken strips in a bowl. Add a pinch of salt and a pinch of cornstarch and cover with water. Leave for 30 minutes.

2 Heat 1 tablespoon of the oil in a wok or deep-sided skillet and stir-fry the chicken for 4 minutes. Transfer the chicken to a warm serving dish and clean the wok or skillet.

3 Heat the remaining oil in the wok and add the garlic, black bean sauce, green and red bell peppers, chile, mushrooms, onions and scallions. Stir-fry the vegetables for 2 minutes, then return the chicken strips to the wok.

4 Add the seasoning ingredients, fry for 3 minutes, and thicken with a little of the cornstarch paste. Serve at once with fresh noodles.

COOK'S TIP

Black bean sauce can be found in specialty shops and in many supermarkets. Use dried noodles if you can't find fresh noodles.

Teppanyaki

This simple, Japanese style of cooking is ideal for thinly sliced breast of chicken. Mirin is a rich, sweet rice wine which is available from Asian shops.

Serves 4

INGREDIENTS

4 boneless chicken breasts
1 red bell pepper
1 green bell pepper
4 scallions

8 baby corn
$1/2$ cup bean sprouts
1 tablespoon sesame or sunflower oil
4 tablespoons soy sauce

4 tablespoons mirin
1 tablespoon grated fresh ginger root

1 Remove the skin from the chicken and slice at a slight angle, to a thickness of about $1/4$ inch.

2 Seed and thinly slice the bell peppers and trim and slice the scallions and corn. Arrange the bell peppers, scallions, corn, and bean sprouts on a plate with the sliced chicken.

3 Heat a large griddle or heavy-based skillet, then lightly brush with oil. Add the prepared vegetables and chicken slices, in small batches, allowing plenty of space between them so that they cook thoroughly.

4 In a small bowl, mix together the soy sauce, mirin, and ginger and serve as a dip with the chicken and vegetables.

VARIATION

If you cannot find mirin add one tablespoons of light brown sugar to the sauce instead.

VARIATION

Instead of serving the sauce as a dip, you could use it as a marinade. However, do not leave the chicken to marinate for more than 2 hours, as the soy sauce will cause it to dry out and become rather tough. Use other vegetables, such as snow peas or thinly sliced carrots, if desired.

Caribbean Chicken

This exotic dish can be made with any cut of chicken, but drumsticks are best for quick and even cooking. Grated fresh coconut adds a delicious, tropical flavor.

Serves 4

INGREDIENTS

8 skinless chicken drumsticks
2 limes
1 teaspoon cayenne pepper
2 medium mangoes

1 tablespoon sunflower oil
2 tablespoons dark brown sugar
lime wedges and fresh parsley,
  to garnish

2 tablespoons coarsely grated
  coconut (optional),
  to serve

1 With a sharp knife, slash the chicken drumsticks at intervals, then place the chicken in a large bowl.

2 Grate the rind from the limes and set aside.

3 Squeeze the juice from the limes and sprinkle over the chicken with the cayenne pepper. Cover and chill in the refrigerator for at least two hours or overnight.

4 Peel the mangoes and chop in half. Discard the stones and cut the flesh into slices.

5 Drain the chicken drumsticks using a slotted spoon and reserve the juice. Heat the oil in a wide heavy pan and sauté the chicken drumsticks, turning frequently, until golden. Stir in the marinade, lime rind, mango slices and the dark brown sugar.

6 Cover the pan and simmer gently, stirring occasionally, for 15 minutes, or until the juices run clear when the chicken is pierced with the point of a sharp knife. Sprinkle with grated coconut, if using, and garnish with lime wedges and fresh parsley.

VARIATION

When buying mangoes, bear in mind that the skin of ripe mangoes varies in color from green to pinky-red, and the flesh from pale yellow to bright orange. Choose mangoes which yield to gentle pressure.

Spanish Chicken with Shrimp

This unusual dish, with its mixture of chicken and shellfish, is typically Spanish. The basis of this recipe is sofrito: a slow-cooked mixture of onion and tomato in olive oil, with garlic and peppers.

Serves 4

INGREDIENTS

4 chicken quarters
1 tablespoon olive oil
1 red bell pepper
1 medium onion
2 garlic cloves, crushed

14 ounce can chopped tomatoes
scant 1 cup dry white wine
4 tablespoons chopped fresh oregano
4¹/₂ ounces chorizo sausage
1 cup peeled shrimp

salt and pepper
rice, to serve

1 Remove the skin from the chicken quarters. Heat the oil in a wide, heavy pan and fry the chicken, turning occasionally, until golden brown.

2 Using a sharp knife, seed and slice the bell pepper and peel and slice the onion. Add the bell pepper and onion to the pan and fry gently to soften.

3 Add the garlic with the tomatoes, wine, and oregano.

Season well with salt and pepper, then bring to a boil, cover, and simmer gently for 45 minutes, or until the chicken is tender and the juices run clear when the thickest part of the chicken is pierced with the point of a sharp knife.

4 Thinly slice the chorizo and add to the pan, together with the shrimp, then simmer for a further 5 minutes. Adjust the seasoning to taste and serve at once with rice.

COOK'S TIP

Chorizo is a spicy Spanish sausage made with pork and a hot pepper, such as cayenne or pimento. It is available from large supermarkets and delicatessens.

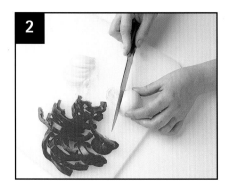

Chicken Korma

Korma is a typically mild and aromatic curry. If you want to reduce the fat in this recipe, use unsweetened yogurt instead of the cream.

Serves 4–6

INGREDIENTS

1 pound 10 ounces chicken meat,
  cut into cubes
1¼ cups double heavy cream
½ teaspoon garam masala

KORMA PASTE:
2 garlic cloves
1-inch piece fresh ginger root,
  coarsely chopped
⅓ cup blanched almonds
6 tablespoons chicken stock
1 teaspoon ground cardamom
4 cloves, crushed
1 teaspoon cinnamon

2 large onions, chopped
1 teaspoon coriander seeds
2 teaspoons ground cumin seeds
pinch cayenne
6 tablespoons olive oil
salt and pepper
cilantro, to garnish

1 Place all the ingredients for the korma paste into a blender or food processor and process until a very smooth paste is formed.

2 Place the cubes of chicken in a bowl and pour the korma paste over them. Stir to coat the chicken completely with the paste. Cover and chill in the refrigerator for 3 hours to allow the flavors to permeate the chicken.

3 Simmer the meat in a large saucepan for 25 minutes, adding a little chicken stock if the mixture becomes too dry.

4 Add the heavy cream and garam masala to the pan and simmer for a further 15 minutes. Allow the korma to stand for 10 minutes before serving. Garnish the chicken korma with fresh cilantro and serve at once with rice.

COOK'S TIP

Garam masala is the mixture of spices commonly used as a base in curries. It can be bought ready-mixed or you can prepare your own by grinding together 1 teaspoon cardamom seeds, 2 teaspoons cloves, 2 tablespoons each cumin seeds and coriander seeds, 3-inch piece cinnamon stick, 1 tablespoon black peppercorns, and 1 dried red chile.

Regal Chicken with Cashew Nut Stuffing

Most of the flavorful stuffing is cooked separately from the chicken, only a small amount is added to the neck end.

Serves 4

INGREDIENTS

1 chicken, weighing about
   3 pounds 5 ounces
1 small onion, halved
2 tablespoons butter, melted
1 teaspoon ground turmeric
1 teaspoon ground ginger
$1/2$ teaspoon cayenne
salt and pepper
fresh cilantro, to garnish

STUFFING:
2 tablespoons oil
1 medium onion, finely chopped
$1/2$ medium red bell pepper,
   finely chopped
2 garlic cloves, crushed
$1/2$ cup basmati rice
$1^1/2$ cups hot chicken stock
grated rind of $1/2$ lemon

$1/2$ teaspoon ground turmeric
$1/2$ teaspoon ground ginger
$1/2$ teaspoon ground coriander
pinch cayenne pepper
$1/2$ cup salted cashews

1 To make the stuffing, heat the oil in a saucepan, add the onion, red bell pepper, and garlic and cook gently for 4–5 minutes. Add the rice and stir to coat in the oil. Add the stock, bring to a boil, then simmer for 15 minutes until all the liquid is absorbed. Transfer to a bowl and add the remaining ingredients for the stuffing. Season well with pepper.

2 Place half the stuffing in the neck end of the chicken and secure with a toothpick. Put the halved onion into the cavity of the chicken. Spoon the rest of the rice stuffing into a greased ovenproof dish and cover with foil.

3 Place the chicken in a roasting pan. Prick all over, avoiding the stuffed area. Mix the butter

and spices, season, then brush over the chicken.

4 Roast in a preheated oven at 375°F for 1 hour, basting the chicken from time to time. Place the dish of rice stuffing in the oven and continue cooking the chicken for 30 minutes. Remove the toothpick and serve the chicken with stuffing and gravy.

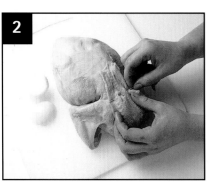

Thai Stir-Fried Chicken with Vegetables

Coconut adds a creamy texture and delicious flavor to this Thai-style stir-fry, which is spiked with green chile.

Serves 4

INGREDIENTS

3 tablespoons sesame oil

12 ounces chicken breast, thinly sliced

2 shallots, sliced

2 garlic cloves, finely chopped

1-inch piece fresh ginger root, grated

1 green chile, finely chopped

1 red bell pepper, thinly sliced

1 green bell pepper, thinly sliced

3 zucchini, thinly sliced

2 tablespoons ground almonds

1 teaspoon ground cinnamon

1 tablespoon oyster sauce

$1/4$ cup creamed coconut, grated

salt and pepper

1 Heat the sesame oil in a wok, add the chicken, season with salt and pepper, and stir fry for about 4 minutes.

2 Add the shallots, garlic, ginger, and chile and stir-fry for 2 minutes.

3 Add the bell peppers and zucchini and cook for about 1 minute.

4 Finally, add the remaining ingredients and seasoning. Stir-fry for 1 minute and serve.

COOK'S TIP

Creamed coconut is sold in blocks by supermarkets and oriental stores. It is a useful storecupboard standby, as it adds richness and depth of flavor.

COOK'S TIP

Since most of the heat of chiles comes from the seeds, remove them before cooking if you want a milder flavor. Be very careful when handling chiles—do not touch your face or eyes, as the chile juice can be very painful. Always wash your hands after preparing chiles.

Golden Chicken Pilau

This is a simple version of a creamy textured and mildly spiced Indian pilau. Although there are lots of ingredients, there's very little preparation needed for this dish.

Serves 4

INGREDIENTS

4 tablespoons butter

8 skinless, boneless chicken thighs, cut into large pieces

1 medium onion, sliced

1 teaspoon ground turmeric

1 teaspoon ground cinnamon

1 cup long grain rice

1³/4 cups plain yogurt

¹/3 cup golden raisins

scant 1 cup chicken stock

1 medium tomato, chopped

2 tablespoons chopped fresh cilantro or parsley

2 tablespoons toasted coconut

salt and pepper

fresh cilantro, to garnish

1 Heat the butter in a heavy or nonstick pan and fry the chicken with the onion for about 3 minutes.

2 Stir in the turmeric, cinnamon, rice, and seasoning and fry gently for 3 minutes.

3 Add the plain yogurt, golden raisins, and chicken stock and mix well. Cover and simmer for

10 minutes, stirring occasionally, until the rice is tender and all the stock has been absorbed. Add more stock if the mixture becomes too dry.

4 Stir in the chopped tomato and chopped fresh cilantro or parsley.

5 Sprinkle the pilau with the toasted coconut and garnish with fresh cilantro.

COOK'S TIP

Long grain rice is the most widely available and the cheapest rice. Basmati, with its slender grains and aromatic flavor is more expensive and should be used on special occasions if it is not affordable on a frequent basis. Rice, especially basmati, should be washed thoroughly under cold, running water before use.

Kashmiri Chicken

This warming, rich, and spicy dish is based on the traditional cooking style of Northern India, using chicken on the bone.

Serves 4

INGREDIENTS

4 skinless chicken drumsticks
4 skinless chicken thighs
$2/3$ cup unsweetened yogurt
4 tablespoons Tikka curry paste
2 tablespoons sunflower oil
1 medium onion, thinly sliced

1 garlic clove, crushed
1 teaspoon ground cumin
1 teaspoon finely chopped fresh
  ginger root
$1/2$ teaspoon chili paste
4 teaspoons chicken stock

2 tablespoons ground almonds
salt
fresh cilantro, to garnish
pilau rice, pickles, and poppadums,
  to serve

1 Slash the chicken fairly deeply at intervals with a sharp knife and place in a large bowl.

2 Mix together the unsweetened yogurt and curry paste and stir into the chicken, tossing to coat evenly. Cover and chill for at least 1 hour.

3 Heat the oil in a large pan and fry the onion and garlic for 4–5 minutes, until softened but not browned.

4 Stir in the cumin, ginger, and chili paste and cook gently for 1 minute.

5 Add the chicken pieces and fry gently, turning from time to time, for about 10 minutes, or until evenly browned. Stir in any remaining marinade with the stock and almonds.

6 Cover the pan and simmer gently for a further 15 minutes or until the chicken is completely cooked and tender.

7 Season to taste with a little salt. Garnish the chicken with cilantro and serve with pilau rice, pickles and poppadums.

VARIATION

If you prefer, use boneless chicken breasts instead of legs, and cut into large chunks for cooking.

Cumin-spiced Apricot Chicken

Spiced chicken legs are partially boned and packed with dried apricots for an intense fruity flavor. A golden, spiced, reduced-fat yogurt coating keeps the chicken moist and tender.

Serves 4

INGREDIENTS

4 large, skinless chicken leg quarters
finely grated rind of 1 lemon
1 cup dried apricots
1 tablespoon ground cumin
1 teaspoon ground turmeric

1/2 cup reduced fat unsweetened
  yogurt
salt and pepper

TO SERVE:
1 1/2 cups brown rice

2 tablespoons slivered hazelnuts
  or almonds, toasted
2 tablespoons sunflower seeds,
  toasted
lemon wedges
salad

1 Remove any excess fat from the chicken legs.

2 Use a small sharp knife to carefully cut the flesh away from the thigh bone.

3 Scrape the meat away down as far as the knuckle. Grasp the thigh bone firmly and twist it to break it away from the drumstick.

4 Open out the boned part of the chicken and sprinkle

with lemon rind and pepper. Pack the dried apricots into each piece of chicken. Fold over to enclose, and secure with toothpicks.

5 Mix together the cumin, turmeric, yogurt, and salt and pepper, then brush this mixture over the chicken to coat evenly. Place the chicken in an ovenproof dish or roasting pan and bake in a preheated oven at 375°F for about 35–40 minutes, or until the juices run clear, not pink, when the chicken is pierced through the

thickest part with the point of a sharp knife.

6 Meanwhile, cook the rice in boiling, lightly salted water until just tender, then drain well. Stir the hazelnuts or almonds and sunflower seeds into the rice. Serve the chicken at once with the nutty rice, lemon wedges and a fresh salad.

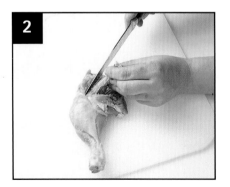

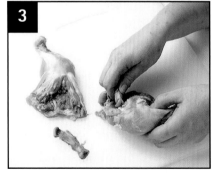

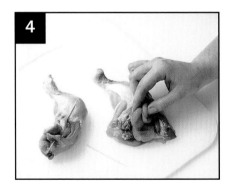

Chili Coconut Chicken

This tasty Thai-style dish has a classic sauce of lime, peanuts, coconut, and chili.
You'll find coconut cream in most supermarkets or delicatessens.

Serves 4

INGREDIENTS

$2/3$ cup hot chicken stock
$1/3$ cup coconut cream
1 tablespoon sunflower oil
8 skinless, boneless chicken thighs,
   cut into long, thin strips
1 small red chili, thinly sliced

4 scallions, thinly sliced
4 tablespoons smooth or crunchy
   peanut butter
finely grated rind and juice of 1 lime

scallion flower and red chili,
   to garnish
boiled rice, to serve

1 Place the chicken stock in a pitcher and crumble the creamed coconut into the stock, stirring to dissolve.

2 Heat the oil in a wok or large heavy skillet and cook the chicken strips, stirring, until golden brown.

3 Add the sliced red chili and the scallions to the wok or skillet and cook gently for a few minutes, stirring to mix all the ingredients.

4 Add the peanut butter, coconut cream, lime rind, and juice and simmer uncovered, stirring, for about 5 minutes.

5 Serve with boiled rice, garnished with a scallion flower and a red chili.

VARIATION

Serve jasmine rice with this spicy dish. It has a fragrant aroma that is well-suited to Thai-style recipes.

VARIATION

Limes are used frequently in Thai cookery, particularly in conjunction with sweet flavors, such as coconut or peanut. They are used in preference to lemons because they have a more acidic flavor, which lends freshness and tartness to many dishes. If limes are unavailable, you can use lemons instead.